Afton

REMEMBERED

Afton
REMEMBERED

Edwin G. Robb

AFTON HISTORICAL SOCIETY PRESS

AFTON, MINNESOTA

The Afton Historical Society Press is a non-profit
organization that takes great pride and pleasure in publishing
fine books on Minnesota subjects.

W. Duncan MacMillan, president
Patricia Condon Johnston, publisher

Cover: Afton's Fourth of July parade going both ways. On the left, heading south on
St. Croix Trail, Don Groth is driving his 1921 Model T Ford Touring Car. Returning
north along the same route is Lucy McAllister's Afton Schooner Band. The building
in the background is the Afton Historical Museum.

Half title page: Looking west toward Afton from Catfish Bar.

Frontispiece: Steamboats at the Afton pasture, now the site of the Afton Marina and
Yacht Club.

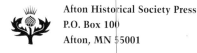

Afton Historical Society Press
P.O. Box 100
Afton, MN 55001

PUBLISHER'S NOTE

I am truly delighted to have helped bring *Afton Remembered* to print. Afton is a place above all others that I cherish. My husband Charlie and I have made Afton our home since 1968 and brought up our four children here.

We built our home on land that once belonged to Afton pioneer Tom Cooney and bought eggs from two of the Berglund brothers who still lived on their Oak Grove farm. Charlie had his first one-man art exhibit at the Berry Patch gallery in the old Afton Citizens' State Bank Building. All three of our daughters worked at the Afton House restaurant in what was once the 1860s Cushing Hotel; Patty waited tables, Jane was a salad girl, and Mary Susan got her first job singing there. Recently, much to our satisfaction, our son Chuck moved back to Afton with his wife Kelly and their son Sam.

This book reflects my fervent hope that by exploring Afton's past, we who prize her present reserve can better understand her homespun character. Afton was built on honest country values, and a country girl she remains. With our help, perhaps she can continue her uncluttered existence into the twenty-first century. The center of the universe for many of us, she deserves no less, and our children will thank us for protecting their legacy.

Publication of *Afton Remembered* was made possible by
generous grants from Charles H. Bell, Lucy and John Hartwell,
and the David Winton Bell Foundation.

Additional contributions to help defray publishing costs were received from Oscar and Beryl Blomgren, Alburta Burns, George Deeks Carroll, William and Betty Lu Crocombe, Dr. A.W. and Dorothy Diessner, Caroline F. Davidson, Donald and Arvonne Fraser, Dick Herreid, Edwin and Debbie Jankura, Mitzi Olson, Dave and Babette Robb, Walter and Jean Robb, Robert and Jeanne Schmitt, and Mary Ellen Sigmond.

To all of you, thank you for your confidence in the Afton Historical Society Press. We are extremely grateful for your support.

Patricia Condon Johnston
April 1996

EARLY FLYER JOYCE SOMMERDORF LATER WORKED AS THE PROPERTY MANAGER FOR THE BELWIN OUTDOOR EDUCATIONAL LABORATORY IN AFTON.

CONTENTS

PREFACE

This is the first history of our little river settlement. Until now, Afton's history lay scattered in bits and pieces within various books, newspapers, pamphlets, and, of course, within the memories of our older natives. No effort had been made to gather these fragments into a unified, coherent whole. And along with all local historians, we were nagged by one, special problem: about the time we were ready to plumb the memories of our still-lucid older residents, both they and their memories had often departed. Feeling grateful for the few occasions we could reverse this trend, we did the best we could.

Certain efforts and events led up to this book. Beginning in the 1970s, sensing the richness of Afton's past, Afton resident Richard Dieter had researched and written informative articles for *The Afton Citizens' Forum Bulletin*. After Mr. Dieter's death in 1991, it seemed appropriate that the Afton Historical Society continue this work. Right about this time, Peggy Gunderson also launched *The Afton Paper*. Peggy has a strong interest in local history and saw her publication as the right vehicle to disseminate it. As a result, my sketches have appeared monthly in *The Afton Paper* since June 1992. It was these articles that prompted publisher Patricia Condon Johnston of the Afton Historical Society Press to suggest that I write this book.

My goal has been to record Afton's story accurately, but since what we blithely call history can sometimes slip into "agreed-upon inaccuracies," we therefore respectfully request anyone who questions or can add to this account to step forward and assist us. Still untold ancestral anecdotes and family genealogies will further enrich what we have set down here as our first efforts.

Many people helped bring this book to fruition. I am particularly grateful to Sandy Berglund, Afton Historical Museum Curator, who was my needed morale builder through moments of doubt. Sandy patiently read the manuscript and made several valuable revisions; she has a wide knowledge of Afton's past, far beyond her years. The following people, nearly all of whom lived in Afton at one time or another, also contributed to the telling of this story: Loraine B. Allen, Barton Anderson, Eunice Anderson, Hubert and Irene Bahnemann, David Berglund, Donald Berglund, Harold Berglund, John Billy, Beryl Blomgren, Dawson Bradshaw, William Broecker, Hazel M. Briggs, Clara J. Clothier, George and Virginia Clymer, Luella Clymer, Sally Cournoyer,

SPREEMAN BOATWORKS, 1921. FRANK SPREEMAN, SR., BUILT ALL TWENTY-SIX OF HIS FLAT-BOTTOMED FISHING BOATS IN A LITTLE SHED NEXT TO HIS OCTAGON HOUSE.

Betty Lu Crocombe, George and Catherine Eastwood, Charlotte Farago, Robert Farnham, Caroline Farnham Davidson, Suzanne Flinsch, Darlene S. Friedrich, Rose O. Hendrickson, Ruby S. Henning, Jack and Emma Herrick, Bruce Johnson, Doris Johnson, Ella S. Johnson, Vacil Kalinoff, Viliss Granberg Kallstrom, Pat B. Keppers, Charles King, Lorraine Lind, Randy Lofgren, Grant McKean, Dr. Roger Meisner, C.R. Mills, Elvina Mueller, Grace R. Nelson, Douglas Nelson, Randy Nelson, Robert Nelson, David Quammen, Harvey Richert, Babette J. Robb, Steve Rosas, Edna Rosenquist, Marion Schmegal, Rev. William Schonebaum, Mary Ellen Sigmond, Harold Sill, Barbara Smith, Kenneth Spreeman, Marcella S. Spreeman, Roy Spreeman, Vernon Spreeman, Ferdinand and Bernice Stoltzmann, and Katherine N. White.

Most of the material about Jacob Fahlstrom was taken from "The Swede Indian" by my mother, Esther Chapman Robb, which appeared in *The Swedish Historical Foundation Yearbook* for 1960.

HOMETOWN MUSICIANS MARTIN LOFGREN, FRANK SPREEMAN, SR., AND WILLIAM LOFGREN PLAYED FOR DANCES ABOUT 1900.

The majority of the vintage photographs are from the Afton Historical Museum. Additional photographs were supplied by Loraine B. Allen, David and Gloria Haslund, Tony Jambor, and Sandy Berglund. For the portrait of Jacob Fahlstrom, we are indebted to the American Swedish Institute of Minneapolis. Several present-day photographs as well as the cover photo, which shows Afton's Fourth of July parade going both ways (in 1994), are the work of Charles J. Johnston.

INTRODUCTION

Just south of Lake St. Croix, the widest part of the lower St. Croix River, Afton lies placidly on its western banks. St. Paul, Minnesota's capital, is twenty freeway miles west; Stillwater, Washington County's seat, is twelve miles upriver. Hudson and Prescott, Wisconsin, are equidistant north and south on the river. Afton's Minnesota suburban neighbors to the north are St. Mary's Point, Lake St. Croix Beach, Lakeland, and Lakeland Shores; Denmark lies south, and Woodbury west.

The St. Croix itself is a clean river of inspiring beauty varying from a half-mile to a mile wide, characterized by an abundance of fine sand bars. The most impressive of these, northeast across the river from Afton, is legendary Catfish Bar—a long, narrow point of sand that curves out from the Wisconsin shore just where the river turns from west to south in its great onward sweep.

An Indian legend about Catfish Bar tells of a warrior returning home from battle who broke a tribal taboo against eating any food en route. Sorely tempted by hunger while stopping to rest at Catfish Bar, he caught a fish for a quick meal. The next morning the hapless sinner was transformed into a giant catfish and covered with sand. Today, people say you can still see the catfish slowly swish its tail as the wind and waves change the direction of the tip of sand at the end of the bar.

An abundance of Indian artifacts have been found on both sides of the river. In our little Robb family garden at Catfish Bar, we found a tomahawk blade and several arrowheads. Afton also contains several Indian mounds, not all of them recorded. The best-known among them are two mounds just south of the present Afton Post Office on 34th Street and St. Croix Trail.

The first white men in the St. Croix Valley were Frenchmen led by Daniel Greysolon, Sieur du Luth, an officer of Governor Frontenac's guard in Quebec. In June 1680 this small expedition paddled and portaged two canoes from Lake Superior into Lake St. Croix, and from there by the ever-widening stream to the Mississippi. Their goal was trade with the Indians in uncharted territory that became Minnesota. According to one source, the St. Croix River is named for a French trader named Sainte-Croix whose boat was wrecked near the conflux of that river and the Mississippi at Prescott.

Following treaties signed by the United States government with the Indians in 1837, French Canadians from the Red River Valley settled at the mouth of Bolles Creek in Afton. These French Canadians did not raise crops as farmers, but they subsisted by gardening. In the 1930s, while wading in Bolles Creek, Afton historian David Haslund discovered an ancient, rusty gun on the sandy bottom. The Minnesota State Historical Society confirmed that this was indeed a French firearm from the 1700s.

Next to arrive in this valley, many of them before 1850, were New Englanders for whom the area pleasantly resembled home. These shrewd Yankees saw huge, potential profits in Minnesota and Wisconsin timber. Following on their heels, in the 1860s and '70s were German immigrants. These people tended to settle not along the river but on the western highlands where the rich soil invited farming. The Germans were followed in record numbers by Swedes who, like the Germans, were encouraged by the Homestead Act to sink down roots here.

The first large-scale business in the St. Croix Valley was lumber, dominated by the sturdy New Englanders. Most of Afton's sawmills were short-lived enterprises, however. In 1854 the Lowery Brothers erected a sawmill at the village, cut one hundred thousand feet of lumber, then closed down and sold their machinery. The next year Thomas and Sons from Indiana built a second sawmill in the village that they operated three seasons; and the Tilton-Newman sawmill built in 1857 also lasted three years. The longer-lived Glenmont sawmill, built in 1857 across the river from Afton, was also considered an Afton enterprise. Then in 1861, the Getchells erected a sawmill in South Afton which burned in 1876.

In 1914, the same year that the region's great white pine forests were exhausted, Afton truck farmers organized the Afton Fruit and Farm Produce Association as a co-operative venture. Strawberries, raspberries, currants, and gooseberries were picked and brought by the crate to "the shed" or "Afton Berry Market" and then to the larger market in St. Paul. Picking the fruit busied residents of all ages. The business reached its maximum profitability just after World War I. Then drought and the Depression, plant disease, and soil exhaustion all took their toll on this home industry so that by the beginning of World War II, it had entirely disappeared.

The present city of Afton comprises both the former village and township. The original riverside village of Afton was a mere six by ten blocks or four-tenths of a mile in area. Town founders R. Haskell, Joseph Haskell, H.L. Thomas, and Charles S. Getchell signed the papers which legalized the tiny political entity. Five north-south streets were platted on the original map—High (now Pennington), Main (Perrot), Washington (St. Croix Trail), Front, and Water. The old Front and Water streets have all but disappeared with the growth of the marinas.

Afton township, platted in 1858, the year Minnesota achieved statehood, comprised a twenty-four square-mile area. While the village was governed by a mayor and trustees, the township elected a chairman and supervisors. Following the merger of the village and township in 1970, the new city of Afton was divided into four wards; each ward elects a council member, and a mayor is elected from the city at large.

In 1880, the first year for which figures are available, the combined population of Afton Village and Afton Township was 925. It peaked at 2,100 in 1910, then began to drop before World War I. Following the Second World War, people from the Twin Cities gradually discovered the St. Croix River, and Afton has ever since experienced growth. For example, in 1960 Afton claimed 1,186 residents in both village and township. By 1970 the population had climbed to 1,993, in 1980 to 2,550, in 1990 to 2,645, and in 1994 to an estimated 2,816.

AFTON RESIDENT GEORGE BRIGGS AND RASPBERRY PICKERS. THE BERRY BUSINESS FLOURISHED IN AFTON FROM AT LEAST THE 1870S.

CATFISH BAR

n 1913 my parents, Walter and Esther Robb, chose for their honeymoon a little rented cottage on the St. Croix River at St. Mary's Point, a settlement just north of Afton. With a spirit of adventure, they had boarded a train in Minneapolis, where they were both born, rode to Stillwater, rented a rowboat, and rowed downriver. Thus began the Robb family's lifelong attachment to the St. Croix River.

Thirteen years later, when the George Melvin Deeks house at Catfish Bar across the river was for sale, my father saw it as a good vacation escape from his aldermanic post and insurance business in Minneapolis. He also knew that it would be an ideal environment in which to raise a family.

Consequently, with two older brothers and a younger sister, I was blessed with almost thirty summers of living in a paradise for young people. My brother Wally once remarked, "If Dad had given each of us a million dollars, it wouldn't have meant as much to us as growing up on the St. Croix."

From 1926, when we moved in, until the end of World War II, only five summer cottages perched beneath that vast bluff known as "Rattlesnake Hill." All of these places were situated at the base of Catfish Bar. Besides our family, the others owning or renting in that little settlement were the Frasers, the Bisbees, the Woolseys, and the

THE DEEKS HOME WALTER ROBB BOUGHT IN 1926 WAS CALLED BILLIKEN LODGE, MEANING THE GOD OF THINGS AS THEY OUGHT TO BE, A POPULAR 1920S COMMERCIAL PROMOTION. INSET: OUR FAMILY DOG PAL, MYSELF (ED ROBB), AND PLAYMATES MARY AND ALAN BISBEE ABOUT 1929.

FROM THE END OF CATFISH BAR, LOOKING EAST TO RATTLESNAKE HILL IN THE FALL, SOME OF THE EDGEMONT HOMES ARE BARELY VISIBLE.

Nicholses. The Frasers, like our family, were from Minneapolis, and the others wintered in St. Paul. Everett Fraser was Dean of the University of Minnesota Law School. Howard Woolsey represented the Waldorf Paper Company; his in-laws, the Bisbees, sold lighting fixtures from their downtown St. Paul store. Dr. Arthur Nichols served as chief health officer for the city of St. Paul.

We called our community Edgemont because it was just north of Glenmont, the site of an old sawmill. Our families were good neighbors and shared beach suppers, organized a small orchestra, and boat-pooled on the daily trips to Afton and back for groceries and mail.

As people on the point, our common way of referring to Catfish Bar, we were aware of the threat it posed to riverboat pilots, most of whom piloted the big

government steamers and barges maintaining the river's channel lights and buoys. Their powerful searchlights often awakened us late at night as they trained them on the bar to make sure they did not run aground. The Coast Guard was responsible for keeping the point itself illuminated, and over the years, several kinds of lights marked its presence, from flashing battery lamps on scaffolds to kerosene lantern buoys. The lantern buoys required an Afton resident to row out each evening before sundown, trim the wick, fill the tank, and relight the lantern.

One of these light tenders was local fisherman Bert Spreeman. The Nels Rosenquist family also took on this job, which paid from nine to thirty dollars a month during the 1930s and early 1940s. Afton resident Ron Rosenquist, Nels's grandson, still owns one of the ancient lanterns which rocked to and fro in the channel, summer after summer, a small contraption doing an immense job.

My earliest memory of Afton reaches back to Spreeman's Landing (now the Windmill Marina managed by Joe Riley and boasting a big fleet of pleasure boats). It was from here that Wisconsin farmer and handyman Charles Holberg rowed our family across the river in 1926 to see the house my father had bought. Nothing more existed at the landing in those days but a small scattering of flat-bottomed boats, a shed, and a minnow tank.

FRANK SPREEMAN, SR., THE OWNER OF SPREEMAN'S LANDING, WAS A GERMAN IMMIGRANT AND THE FATHER OF A LARGE FAMILY. SPREEMAN PAINSTAKINGLY CRAFTED HIS BOATS AND OARS IN A WORK SHED AT THE BACK OF THE SPREEMAN FAMILY'S ALREADY HISTORIC OCTAGON-SHAPED HOME.

Frank Spreeman's boat-rental business drew fishermen from a wide area, especially the Twin Cities, and Old Frank, forever sloshing about in his rubber hip boots, spent his days dispatching his boats, moving them here and there, and fastening their chains to stakes. After rainstorms, Frank bailed out his boats with tin cans; the sound of metal scraping against wood always followed a downpour.

In his later years, Frank became nearly stone deaf. Fond of jokes, he told them at full volume. On a quiet day we could hear his laughter clear across the river as he slapped his hip-booted thigh and roared, "By golly, that's a good one."

Eventually, Frank sold his business to his son Bert (whose given name was Albert). Bert and his brother, Frank Spreeman, Jr., were commercial fishermen. Using a huge seine, the brothers had made the largest catch of carp and sheephead ever taken from the St. Croix; in April 1915, they caught 16,250 pounds of fish which they sold for $1,300 to the Lakeside Ocean Company in Chicago.

I remember seeing Bert and Frank one time years later, making a huge haul like that on Catfish Bar, the sinewy cords and muscles of their arms bulging as they cranked the handles of the winches that pulled in the nets filled with flopping fish.

Another of Frank, Sr.'s sons, Emil, was nicknamed "Spike" and became a jeweler in Stillwater. Emil was one of the early owners of the property where the Charlie Bell family of Wayzata later developed the Belwin Outdoor Educational Laboratory.

Just north of the Spreeman landing was a riverside pasture that, much like the soothing green pastures in the Twenty-Third Psalm, lay in deep shadows by late afternoon. In earlier times, steamboats had landed here, bringing both freight and passengers. In my time, the pasture was where Afton's winning baseball team, the Red Socks, encountered its rivals from neighboring towns in many do-or-die contests of skill. Some of the stars were Bert Spreeman, Mickey Picullel, Roy Johnson, Tony Hedstrom, Tony Nord, and Bert Baskin.

This pasture also served as an early airstrip. From across the river on Catfish Bar, we

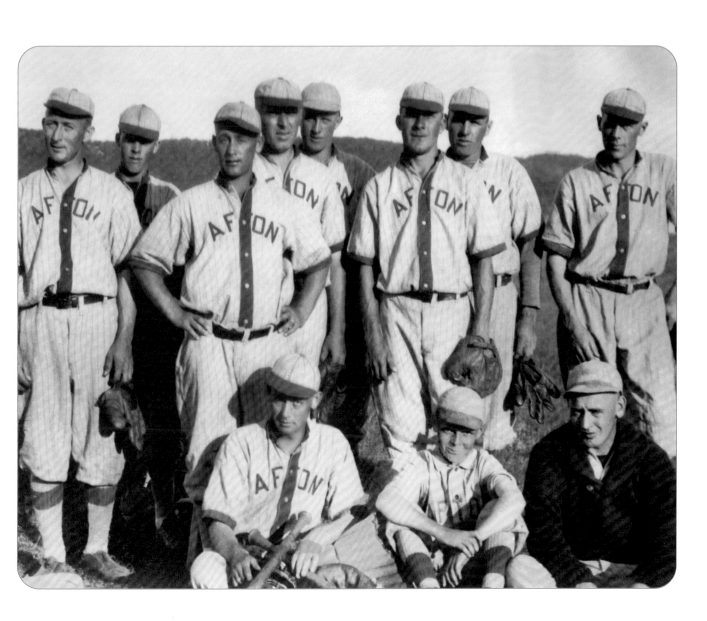

could sometimes see a biplane piloted by Afton native Roy Johnson taking off or landing, bouncing along the bumpy runway. Johnson had been a World War I navy fighter pilot and later became mayor of Afton, then Washington County auditor for thirty years beginning in 1936.

Although my family came here three years before the Afton Citizens' State Bank failed in 1929, the Afton of my youth already had a down-at-the-heel look with its gravel paths and motley collection of unpainted stores and houses. It was not visually attractive.

The focal point of village businesses was the square, brick building erected in 1913 across a side road from the present Afton House Inn. This structure remained essentially unchanged as it evolved from bank to hardware store and post office to grocery store. In the 1970s and 1980s it housed an art gallery and the Berry Patch Loft, a yarn shop. Boasting two plate-glass windows, this early bank building was Afton's second brick structure, the first being the brick school at the north edge of the park.

I am old enough also, to hold a vivid recollection of the serviceable, unpainted berry shed to the east of the brick bank building. Driving our family car into the shed, we were helped by, among others, Clarence or Nels Lind or Melvin Hendrickson who loaded crates of strawberries or raspberries into the back seat because we had no trunks in those days. We exited the shed to the south between the barbershop and the garage, delighted to have bought some of Afton's superb fruit.

During our brief visits to town, we youngsters from the Wisconsin shore came to know and admire the village smithy, Chris Christensen. Hiking from Spreeman's landing to the Richert store we passed by Chris's shop, which was north of Selma's Ice Cream Parlor. Stepping inside the double doors, we watched Chris pound the red-hot horse shoes on the anvil while the horse casually stomped its feet. Chris's wife, Augusta Olson Christensen, or "Gussie" to villagers, played the old pump organ with grim determination at the Afton Methodist Church for fifty-eight years.

Afton had some colorful denizens in those days. There was "Gramma" Mathilda Olson Picullel, for instance, with her pronged nose and dentureless gums smiling from beneath her little flowered bonnet; we would see her in the Richert store, snatching flies out of the air and squishing them between her little hands. Mrs. Picullel's father-in-law, John Picullel, had been one of the founders of the Swedish Evangelical Lutheran Church.

Also arresting in appearance was Mike Kelly, who owned a generous mat of white hair and the Minneapolis Millers baseball team. "Kel's Coulee" at the south end of the village traces its present name to this florid-faced, high-spirited Irishman who summered on the River Road.

Another unforgettable character was six-foot, slow-witted Otto Parson. Otto had come to Afton from Sweden with his parents in 1880, and, like his father, worked at the

Glenmont sawmill across the river from the family home. Often teased by his peers, Otto would occasionally explode and scare up some measure of respect. When Otto's wife Ella died, he reportedly wore her monkey fur coat to her funeral at the Afton Methodist Church and interrupted the service to pay the preacher.

But the most unforget-table man of all, perhaps, was John Birger Carlson, another Swede, arriving in Afton as a young man. Carlson, who had been a gardener for Leland Stanford in Palo Alto, California, pronounced his initials "Jay Bay Say" and was considered a dandy by the ladies. Dressing in white shirt, tie, and white duck pants and spats, he could always be counted upon as a partner for the unescorted ladies at village dances.

Sadly, Carlson's clothing and hygiene diminished year by year, and he ended his days a raggedy little, old

JOHN BIRGER CARLSON WITH MAUDE SILVER, A FRIEND OF GEORGE DEEKS, THE MAN WHO BUILT THE HOUSE MY PARENTS PURCHASED ON CATFISH BAR.

septuagenarian. The last summers of his life, I'd see him rowing the old, patched-up flat-bottomed boat that Bert Spreeman had given him. He'd row to Edgemont where the kindly housewives would give him a bit of breakfast and coffee. Then he'd poke through their garbage cans for bits of food to take back to the tiny, shed-like shelter in Afton he called home. Despite his pathetic condition, John's instincts were decent, and he would often take the Catfish Bar folks boxes of berries he had picked.

GIANTS ON THE LAND

Afton pioneer Joseph Haskell was Minnesota's first farmer. Born in 1805 at Greene, Massachusetts, he lived for a time in Indiana and Missouri before boarding the steamer *Ariel* for Fort Snelling in July 1839. Arriving in the untamed Northwest, this well-read Yankee worked briefly for early lumberman and entrepreneur Franklin Steele at St. Croix Falls, Wisconsin, before laying claim to Section 25 of the future Afton Township. In the autumn, he and a companion, James S. Norris, broke three acres of sod with four yoke of oxen and a cast-iron plow in preparation for the spring planting of corn and potatoes. Imagine their jubilation when in 1840 they harvested the first crops north of Prairie du Chien, Wisconsin.

In 1841 Norris began his own farm seven miles southwest of Afton in Cottage Grove where he reportedly became Minnesota's first wheat farmer. Seven years later, Haskell returned east for his three sisters—Mary, Clara, and Saphira Jane—who kept house for him in Afton until he married Olive Kingman Furber in 1849. Joseph and Olive Haskell parented four children; their firstborn, Helen, was the first white child born in Afton Township. Not surprisingly, James Norris married Haskell's sister Saphira Jane.

Indians came often to the Haskell farm. Frequently they brought game to cook on the stove, and they sometimes feasted and caroused all night while Haskell slept in an adjoining room. After Olive came to the farm, Haskell felt comfortable leaving her alone all day until, during one of his absences, an Indian entered the house pretending to beg for food. When the intruder made a threatening move toward Olive, she chased him out with a butcher knife. Upon returning, Joseph became so enraged he left the house, rifle at the ready, determined to destroy any Indians he might find in the woods. "Fortunately for everyone," wrote son Hiram Haskell in his pamphlet, *Joseph Haskell of Afton*, "he found none."

An educated man with a teacher's certificate (from Bangor, Maine), who had come west with a small but select collection of books and magazines, Joseph Haskell was active

THE JOSEPH HASKELL FARM HOME ON TRADING POST TRAIL WAS BUILT IN THE 1860S AND TORN DOWN IN 1955. INSET: JOSEPH HASKELL'S WIFE, OLIVE KINGMAN FURBER HASKELL ABOUT 1880.

25

in politics and education on many levels. Elected a commissioner in Washington County's first election in 1849, with Afton town fathers James Getchell, H.L. Thomas, and G.W. Cutler, he helped plat Afton Village in 1855 and Afton Township in 1858. After starting Afton Township's first school in his home in 1855, as a member of the state legislature from 1869 to 1871, he was instrumental in establishing the state's first Normal School at Winona and served on its board of directors.

When Joseph Haskell died in 1885, the first farm in Minnesota passed to his children amid some litigation. Subsequent owners have included Harold Broecker, who held the farm from 1920 until 1937; Robert and Betty Rosas, who replaced the old, rundown house with a new one in 1961; and present owners James and Suzanne Flinch. Eighty acres of the farm are still being tilled today.

A second Afton pioneer agriculturist, John William Boxell, planted one of Minnesota's first orchards and vineyards. Born in 1824 in Ohio, Boxell, like, Haskell, was well-schooled; he had taken post-graduate courses, taught college classes, and written a highly praised mathematics textbook. After marrying Mary Shaw in 1848, he combined managing his father William's farm, teaching school in the winter, and serving as a lieutenant in the Ohio State Militia. Upon the death of his father in 1853, he sold the family farm and brought his wife, his mother, and his three sons to Valley Creek, about three miles northwest of Afton Village, where he bought eighty acres along the creek.

Although the Afton Berry Association was not formed until 1914, some fifteen years after Boxell's death, we feel safe in calling him the "Father of Afton's berry business." It is hard to imagine that the local growers of strawberries, raspberries, blackberries, currants, and gooseberries did not take their cue and benefit from Boxell's excellent, pioneering work in horticulture.

Boxell and his wife Mary won countless awards and wide recognition for their produce

THE JOHN AND MARY BOXELL FAMILY AT HOME. DESCENDANTS HAVE CALLED THEIR UNCLES ROB AND JIM THE FAMILY CUT-UPS, AND TOLD OF THEIR CLIMBING INTO THE BELL TOWER OF THE NEW ST. CROIX VALLEY ACADEMY AND INSCRIBING THEIR INITIALS ON THE LARGE BEAMS. SURE ENOUGH, IN THIS PICTURE, IT IS ROB AND JIM WHO SIGNAL MISCHIEF FROM THEIR UPSTAIRS WINDOW PERCH.

at both the Washington County and Minnesota State fairs. Some of their ribbons are displayed at the Afton Historical Museum. Commenting on the couple's 105 varieties of seeds and their preserves and jellies on September 13, 1874, the *Minneapolis Daily Tribune* praised their exhibit as "altogether the best ever seen at the State Fair in Minnesota."

About 1859 John Boxell started on his own land a private school, located just across the road from the historic Bahneman farm where Irene Bahneman, widow of Hubert Bahneman, still lives. (Hubert's grandfather, Martin Bahneman, came to Valley Creek in 1865.) Unfortunately, this school lasted only a few years before it was destroyed by fire, the victim of a bizarre accident. One frigid night a tramp, unable to find shelter, homed in on the school. Stoking the stove with chunks of wood too big for it, the trespasser soon had a fire that roared out of control. He just barely escaped as the modest structure burned to the ground. After the fire, Boxell taught school for several years in his home.

Eleven children were born to John and Mary Boxell including twin daughters who were both born and died in July 1869. Following the Civil War, in which he served with the Minnesota Volunteers, Boxell helped found the St. Croix Valley Academy in 1867. Not only did all seven Boxell sons graduate from the academy, but three of them—Robert, John, and Edward—also taught there.

A versatile man of many accomplishments, John Boxell became a prolific magazine writer, contributing articles about horticulture, botany, farming, mathematics, and astronomy. In 1884 the Boxells moved to St. Paul, where he continued writing until his

SEED BEDS AT THE MAY NURSERY IN TURN-OF-THE-CENTURY AFTON.

death at the age of seventy-one in 1895. Six of his seven sons served as pallbearers at his funeral at Oakland Cemetery in St. Paul.

A third Afton pioneer, Louis Lovell May, started one of the oldest—possibly the first—nursery in the state. Dating to 1899, it occupied about 250 acres in Valley Creek. Several photographs in the Afton Historical Museum show the old L.L. May Nursery as a bustling commercial concern with a small army of men, horses, and equipment, a large building in the background. At the peak of its summer operations, the firm employed 125 men. Using the railroad depot in

Lakeland, the nursery shipped apple trees to farms throughout the state. More importantly, by experimenting with a wide variety of plants to learn which of them would thrive in this region, May expanded the range of plants available to Minnesota gardeners.

The elegant residence inhabited by May and his wife had been built in 1888 by the fifth governor of Minnesota, William Rainey Marshall. Constructed years after Marshall's term in office (1866-1870), it was a grand, southern-style mansion with a two-storied portico, majestic white pillars, and a large central entryway. "There was a long, broad, curving drive up to the door and, to my young eyes, this was the absolute showplace of the area," wrote Valley Creek historian Evelyn Bolles Grant in 1963.

The Marshall-May house fronted the west side of Stage Coach Trail just south of the present Randall "Bud" Nelson farm. A gate, but not the original one, marks the old drive-way leading to the site of the house. Although we do not know when this imposing structure came down, a small trace of it exists in the nearby Jack and Emma Herrick house, where two large windows of three panes each from the mansion have been built into the front porch.

According to Evelyn Grant, an unconfirmed report blamed unlucky speculation by Louis May for the loss of all his holdings. Investing in worthless gold mine stock was said to have caused his financial downfall. Following the Mays on the land came a series of casual stewards and the old nursery deteriorated.

After John and Grace Stoltze purchased the property in 1931, they labored tirelessly to prevent nature from reclaiming the great variety of trees and flowers developed by May. Each year they took aerial pictures of their land in autumn for their Christmas cards. The earlier photographs reveal easily identifiable rows of variegated trees and plants; in later years, however, there is a definite blurring of these rows. The L.L. May Nursery, a happy first in Afton, has receded into history, but much of the beauty of its exotic plant world will remain here forever as a legacy for us to enjoy.

Pioneer Afton also boasted the first Swede in Minnesota, Jacob Fahlstrom, who undoubtedly led the most varied and dramatic life of anyone in our little pantheon. A rough-and-ready personality known to his contemporaries as the "Swede-Indian," he pops in and out of journals, diaries, and letters in a fascinating if fragmentary way; consequently, he has become something of a legend in the triangle of country lying between the Mississippi and St. Croix rivers.

Fahlstrom's life before coming to Afton was the stuff of novels. Born in Sweden in the 1790s, he went to sea at a tender age as a cabin boy on a steamer captained by an uncle. The ship was wrecked on the English coast, and young Jacob escaped to London with his uncle and there became separated from him. Now on his own, he applied to the Swedish consul for aid and was introduced to Lord Selkirk who was organizing a company of men to go to his settlement on the Red River in British North America. Selkirk took the lad with him to the New World, where Fahlstrom found work with the Hudson Bay Company. One day, while out with a hunting party, he became lost in the Canadian wilderness, where he met up with a band of Ojibwa Indians who adopted him into the tribe and called him "Yellow Head." Fahlstrom learned the Indians' language and married a beautiful young Lake Superior Ojibwa woman named Margaret Bungo, said to be the daughter of the tribe's chief.

Next Fahlstrom drifted south to where the Mississippi and the Minnesota rivers meet, perhaps ten years before Fort Snelling was built there in 1820. Later he worked at the fort cutting wood and carrying the mail to Fort Crawford at Prairie du Chien, to St.Croix Falls, Wisconsin, and to the Lake Superior country. These trips of his, wrote W.H.C. Folsom in *Fifty Years in the Northwest*, entailed "many hair-raising escapes from hostile Indians."

In 1837 Fahlstrom was the first Methodist convert in Minnesota, and he took up ministering to the Indians at the Kaposia mission, now the site of South St. Paul. "Father Jacob" also worked with local half-bloods, the growing number of white settlers, and lumberjacks in the northern lumber camps. In 1841 he moved his family, which would include nine children, to Valley Creek on the Indian Trail just south of present Interstate 94. Here the latchstring of his cabin was always out for neighbors, visiting preachers, and circuit riders.

Hanging in the American Swedish Institute in Minneapolis is a portrait of this humble and undistinguished man who did so much to help establish the Methodist Church on the Minnesota frontier. Far from impressive in appearance, he was undersized and stockily built with an unusually large head. Also on display is Jacob Fahlstrom's well-worn, tattered bible, given to him by his mother in Stockholm, which he carried everywhere.

In June 1948 Prince Bertil of Sweden came to Minnesota to unveil a memorial plaque on Kellogg Boulevard in St. Paul commemorating the significant role played by Aftonite Jacob Fahlstrom in opening up and settling the upper Midwest. Little Afton is proud that something about its character apparently appealed to this exceptional man to cause him to choose the area as his final home.

AFTON'S SO-CALLED SWEDE-INDIAN, JACOB FAHLSTROM, WAS THE FIRST SWEDE IN MINNESOTA. FOLLOWING AN EARLY LIFE OF ADVENTURE, FAHLSTROM TOOK UP MISSIONARY WORK AND FARMING IN VALLEY CREEK. KNOWN AS FATHER JACOB'S PLACE, HIS HOME WAS ALWAYS OPEN TO TRAVELERS. FAHLSTROM DIED IN 1857 AND IS BURIED ON A SECLUDED HILLTOP ON HIS HOMESTEAD.

MILLERS AND DIARISTS

Valley Creek in the former Afton Township gives no hint today that it was once a thriving business community. The flour mills, the blacksmith shop, the stores, the post office—all are gone.

More than 150 years ago Valley Creek's commercial activity dawned with Lemuel Bolles from Connecticut, who arrived in Afton at age fifty in 1842. The next spring Bolles constructed a grist mill from timber slabs he salvaged along the lakeshore and hauled to his place on his not-so-young back. Named "Milton Mills," after a town in Bolles's native New England, the Bolles mill was the first privately owned flour mill north of Prairie du Chien, Wisconsin, and a forerunner of the Minneapolis milling industry.

Bolles Creek was named for Lemuel, the first of several Bolles who captured its water power. With a fall of only nine feet and an output of fifty barrels of flour a day, the primitive mill ground corn and wheat. Rev. Edward D. Neill wrote in his *History of Washington County and the St. Croix Valley* that Bolles operated his mill "some time and then transferred it to Christopher Carli, and he to Andrew Mackey, who made some improvements and ran it one year." The last person to own the mill was Emil Munch, who made more changes and named it "Reliance Mill," only to close it down in 1875.

Meanwhile, twenty years after having given the milling industry its start in Minnesota, Lemuel Bolles had come to an unhappy end. Lakeland diarist Mitchell Jackson wrote on Sunday, May 1, 1863: "Evening go down to see old 'Uncle Bolles' who has dropsy pretty badly and to make the matter worse has to be moved out of his old homestead—reason he got in debt and the creditors and lawyers must have it It is a burning shame The old man ought to be left to die upon the place where he has lived and worked hard for nearly a quarter of a century." The pioneer miller was taken to the Sawyer House hotel in Stillwater where he died a few months later.

THE GRIST MILL LEMUEL BOLLES BUILT IN VALLEY CREEK IN 1843. HAVING NO NAILS WITH WHICH TO CONSTRUCT HIS BUILDING, HE USED WOODEN PINS. EXCEPT FOR THE GOVERNMENT MILL AT ST. ANTHONY, LEMUEL'S WAS THE FIRST FLOUR MILL NORTH OF PRAIRIE DU CHIEN, WISCONSIN. LEMUEL BOLLES WAS ALSO AFTON'S FIRST POSTMASTER AT HIS MILTON MILLS IN 1852.

Lemuel's nephew, Erastus Bolles, also settled in Valley Creek, bringing his wife Sophronia and two children here in the 1850s. Erastus operated a blacksmith shop, manufactured farm equipment, opened the second flour mill in Valley Creek (1856), and started the community's first general store. The Bolles children, Emma and Charles, attended John Boxell's private school on Valley Creek Trail. When it burned, their energetic father organized and donated the land for the Bolles or Valley Creek School. This school later became School District 39. Following grade school, Emma and Charles were part of the St. Croix Valley Academy's first class of 130 students.

In the early 1870s, Erastus Bolles sold his mill, blacksmith shop, and manufacturing business to his son Charles—another hard worker like his father and great-uncle Lemuel. Charles's daughter Evelyn Bolles Grant described her father as "a scholarly and well-read man but also an extrovert with quick temper and keen wit." During World War I Charles worked in a defense plant in Stillwater. An excellent musician, he played cornet and drums in the Valley Creek Band, which performed one summer on an excursion steamer cruising between Prescott and Stillwater. At home in the house his father Erastus had built, Charles played the piano and organ in the living room.

WITH THE HELP OF FRIENDLY INDIANS, ERASTUS BOLLES BUILT A HANDSOME, GREEN-SHUTTERED, COLONIAL-STYLE HOUSE. ITS TWO STORIES, TEN ROOMS, L-SHAPE, AND BARE MINIMUM OF GREEK REVIVAL FEATURES MADE IT A VALLEY SHOWPLACE, AND IT LATER BOASTED THE FIRST RUNNING WATER AND TELEPHONE IN VALLEY CREEK. MR. AND MRS. E.A. HERRINGTON NOW OWN THIS STAGE-COACH TRAIL HOUSE.

Charles Bolles married three times. His first two wives died in childbirth. His third wife, Evelyn Grant's mother, was Lillie Harriman Wilcox of Hudson, Wisconsin. The milling business took its tragic toll on Charles as well. During the years, both Erastus and then Charles lost their mills to fire and struggled to rebuild them. Charles accomplished the final mill reconstruction with borrowed capital. Despite his courageous hard work, however, he ended up losing the mill to mortgage foreclosure. Tormented by severe asthma resulting from years in flour milling, and bedridden with a stroke, Charles died at fifty-two in 1933.

In 1943 daughter Evelyn returned from Stillwater with her husband, Jay Grant, to the family home in Afton to care for her mother. "There has been a Bolles in the old house for 120 years," she wrote in her 1963 *History of Valley Creek and Surrounding Community*, justifiably proud of her lineage. After Jay died in the mid-1970s, Evelyn lived on in the house contentedly several more years. Filled with fine old furniture, it was still bordered by roses her grandmother had brought from the East.

The writings of two earlier area residents further illuminate Afton's past. Published by the Minnesota Historical Society in *Minnesota Farmers' Diaries* (1939), the journals of William R. Brown and Mitchell Y. Jackson reveal a broad view of life in this region in the mid-1800s. Both diarists were not only farmers, they also involved themselves in the general development of the territory.

William Reynolds Brown's diary spans a brief eight-month period from October 1845 through June 1846. Born in 1816 in Ohio, Brown was a carpenter before settling in Minnesota at Red Rock, across the Mississippi from the Dakota village of Kaposia. There he erected several buildings and married mission school teacher Martha Boardman. Besides serving as justice of the peace, Brown made his living farming, and there was always a great deal to do.

His first entry, dated October 25 reads: "Finished Harvesting & burying our Rutabagas and flat Turnips weather Remarkably warm and pleasant, smokey & dry." Two days later, on October 2, he "gathered up the pieces of rails & Bark around the fences today put up 2 barrels of ashes to leach Sold our yoke of Steers 2 years old to young Lavicinia for $36 also our pair of yearlings for $16. Hauled up sand and lime for Daubing purposes."

Besides detailing his day-to-day struggles on the farm, Brown recorded his purchases and remarked on his visits and dealings with area residents. Afton pioneers James Norris and Joseph Haskell he mentions repeatedly. On December 13, Brown arrived home to find "a party of our Neighbors there[—]a weding party consisting [of] James S. Norris & Sophia Haskell to be married attended by Joseph Haskell[,] Mrs. Mary Davis & Clara Haskell they arrived at 11 o'clock took dinner tarried until 8 in the evening took supper I married Norris & Sophia & they all went home."

That winter, in January 1846, Brown one day started for Stillwater but ended up spending the night with the Haskells because the road was "Icy & Bad." A few days later, he and Haskell traveled "up the Lake" to Marine Mills, where he bought a "new Cap at 7.00, Martha a Clothes Basket at 1.25, 4 lbs alum 50[,] pint shoe pegs 12½, 4 prs small Butto[ns] .40, 2½ yds flannel 1.62[,] Martha pair shoe[s] 1.25 and some other little articles." Starting for home, Brown and Haskell stopped in Stillwater for dinner with the Greeleys, where "Mrs. Vail" was "playing at Back Gamon & Cards." Brown was not "much please[d]" with Mrs. Vail, adding, "I [think] the Ladies at Stillwater are rather *straining* a point to appear *Refined*."

In March, Brown "Had a very pleasant time" at the wedding of John McHattie and Jane Middleton. "They had Liquor & drank of which I disapproved. We indulged in the simple plays usually played on such occasions I hope the day is not far distant when such things will not be countenanced by the better sort of people We started home at 2 o'clock at night. I saw Mrs. Andy [Mackey] for the first time I think her a good woman." (Andrew Mackey lived in Afton and once owned most of the present business district.)

Taking up his pen slightly later, Lakeland farmer Mitchell Jackson began his diary, which spans almost a decade, in August 1852. Born near Mount Vernon, Ohio, in 1816, Jackson had spent his boyhood on a farm in Indiana and later worked with his father in a warehouse, forwarding, and commission business. In 1855 he brought his wife and two sons to acreage he had selected between Afton and Lakeland, about a half mile west of Lake St. Croix.

The Jacksons were ardent Christians who regularly attended Sunday church services in both Lakeland and Afton. On June 24, 1855, Jackson wrote of attending a church "meeting at Afton a new town laid off by Messrs Getchell[,] Thomas & others 3 or four miles down the lake shore." The occasion was a sad one; Afton was burying "a child of Mr. Stouffer which is the second death in his family within a week from Putrid sore throat."

Afton is mentioned again in Jackson's diary on November 8, 1858, when he writes that he had his horses shod at Afton; and an entry in early spring, 1860, reveals that he went to Afton to pick up his wagon which was being repaired and "to get a wild hive of bees" from local farmer Albert Martin.

During the seventeen years Jackson lived on his Lakeland farm, he was active in Republican party affairs and held several county offices. He rejoiced when Abraham Lincoln, "first Republican ever elected to that office," was sworn into office on Monday, March 4, 1861. "He finds governmental affairs much complicated as some half doz of the slave states have seceeded [sic] and are in open rebellion, their leaders declaring they will not submit to republican rule."

On September 26, Jackson made a sad journey to Newport to see one of his young neighbors off to war: "Mr. Fowler leaves this morning with the rest of the volunteers for the fort He leaves an excellent wife and three small children the youngest not 4 weeks old No wonder our breakfast is eaten in silence Here is an intelligent and conscientious young husband and father about to sever at least for a long time and very likely for ever the dearest earthly ties[.] I wish I could go too."

In December 1870, Mitchell Jackson sold his farm and moved to Iowa. His fellow diarist, William Brown, ended his days in Newport, Minnesota. Remembering them as intelligent, energetic men who helped develop our young republic, we are especially grateful to them for their readable accounts of life along the St. Croix.

THE SCION OF PIONEER NEW ENGLANDERS, MITCHELL YOUNG JACKSON FARMED IN LAKELAND FOR SEVENTEEN YEARS.

TWELVE SCHOOLS

Afton Village and Afton Township together at various times were home to twelve different schools. Historian Edward D. Neill wrote that one of the first steps the pioneers took after building shelters for their families was to provide schools for the children. Just as they formed churches for their spiritual well-being, these newcomers valued education and did not want their children to be deprived of it, even for a short time.

Afton Township's first institution of learning was the Joseph Haskell School, founded in 1855 and named for Minnesota's first farmer. The organizational meeting was held in Haskell's house; elected to its board were Thomas Persons, H.F. Dayton, and Joseph Haskell.

Farmer Jesse Jackson gave the land for this first school in a beautiful grove on section 21. A four-hundred-dollar tax was voted for construction costs, and the school's first three-month session began July 12, 1856. In 1881 Neill noted, "Mr. Oldham has been clerk for twenty-three years."

By 1862 the Haskell School was officially designated School District 23. Thirty-one pupils packed the little school in 1900. The teacher that year was Ella Spence. In time, the little school became known as the "Eastwood School" for pioneer farmer Thomas Eastwood and his wife Alice, on whose land the school was located. Some of the pupils who attended this school and later came back to teach at it included Mrs. Tom Eastwood, and Joe and Will Oldham. They worked for wages ranging from twenty to thirty dollars per month. In the 1940s and 1950s the teachers were Ruth Stucci, Harriet Malberg, her daughter Ruth Malberg Wolfe, and Rebecca Rosenquist.

In 1952 the Haskell-Eastwood School was absorbed into the consolidated Afton-Lakeland School, the new District 22. The old building, now remodeled into a home, still stands in its original location, north of and very close to Highway 95, east of the fork where 95 and Trading Post Trail meet.

Also dating to 1856, the second school and first one in Afton Village was a small frame structure erected on the road leading to Gummeson's Coulee, as it was then called, at the south end of Afton. The coulee's namesake, Clement Gummeson, was a Civil War veteran who died in 1912 and is buried in Afton's Evergreen Cemetery. This deep, beautiful glen is now called "Kel's Coulee" for Afton's baseball czar, Mike Kelly, one-time owner of the Minneapolis Millers.

This school building, which had no special name we know of, became the home of the Mauritz Schelin family. When the little school became too crowded, the extra students were shifted to another small frame building on the corner of St. Croix Trail and 32nd Street, where Bonnie Lind's house now stands.

A third school, this one also in the village, was taught by the Rev. Simon Putnam some time after 1859 in the kitchen of his parsonage, now the Rotzels' "little red house."

In addition to its public schools, Afton for several years claimed a private school. Horticulturist and writer John William Boxell started this school about 1859 on Bolles Creek across Valley Creek Trail from the Hubert and Irene Bahnemann farm.

The fifth school, in the township, was Valley Creek's public school, District 39, organized on April 7, 1863, at the home of the miller on Bolles Creek, Erastus Bolles. Bolles donated the land for the school, and the new schoolhouse was built to the west of County Highway 21 near the present Roger Meisner barn. The first teacher hired by the board of directors headed by Bolles was Miss C.L. Rice. In 1884 Lizzie Cooney, Tom Cooney's sister, taught at the Bolles or Valley Creek School and boarded with Bolles's daughter, Mrs. Silas Geer. Other teachers at Valley Creek in later years were Violet Forceia, Harriet Palm, and Gloria Haslund.

The first Bolles school is rumored to have burned, and it appears that a new school was built in 1890 or 1891 across the road. So many pupils attended here that some of them were transferred to the Afton Township Hall for instruction.

Nor were pioneer Aftonites satisfied with providing only a rudimentary education for their offspring. Concerned that their children's schooling stopped with the eighth grade, Afton citizens called a meeting on December 6, 1867, to consider "the propriety of building an academy." Rev. Alva D. Roe and C.S. Getchell agreed to canvass citizens for construction funds, and within sixty days they had secured pledges for ten thousand dollars to build the St. Croix Valley Academy.

The board of trustees included such familiar names as Rev. Roe, Richard Buswell, W.W. Getchell, L.T. Olds, J. Warren Furber, N.M. Chase, and James Middleton. The Free Masons laid the cornerstone on June 18, 1868, and the school was dedicated that same fall. Neill described the building as a "handsome, three-story brick edifice surmounted with tower and bell." Its interior finished in black walnut and oak, it was "furnished with neat and convenient single desks" and included a music room with pianos and organs.

Among the 130 pupils enrolled in the first class were Charles E. Bolles, Tom Cooney, the future Mr. and Mrs. Thomas Eastwood, and Moses Clapp, who later became a United States senator from Minnesota. The academy's liberal arts curriculum attracted students from as far as St. Paul Park and Newport, some of whom walked to and from the school on weekends.

By 1884, however, enrollment had dropped sharply. Disappointed trustees closed the school and sold the property to a Rev. P. Duborg who presented it to the German Evangelical Lutheran Joint Synod of Ohio for a theological seminary. Afton's seventh school, this seminary opened for classes in January 1885. Rev. Henry Ernst was the German seminary's president and professor of theology. For the nine years of the school's operation, Ernst and his family occupied the octagon house in Afton.

During its short life span, the seminary graduated more than fifty men to serve in the Lutheran ministry. After closing in Afton, the seminary first moved to the Lake Phalen area of St. Paul and then merged with the Wartburg Seminary in Waverly, Iowa. Through more reorganization, it finally became part of the American Lutheran Church. With the academy and seminary defunct, the solid, yellow brick building was purchased for one thousand dollars from the Ohio Synod for Afton's eighth school, School District 24.

Afton farmer and historian Alvin Hedstrom has left some choice descriptions of the teachers in this historic building, the village's first commodious school quarters. In a 1951 *Stillwater Gazette* column, Hedstrom wrote, "Miss Flynn was an attractive and personable young woman with red hair and a temper to match. She always carried a short, light rod with which to enforce rules and obedience. She taught in 1892." There was also E. N. Swanson, farmer and teacher, a tall and muscular man, "who could take a boy in each hand, lift them off the floor, and bang their heads together."

In my own memory, teachers at Afton's public school in the old academy included Alice Peterson before World War II, Marian Broecker from 1941 to 1943, and Anna Johnson and Katherine Rafferty after the war.

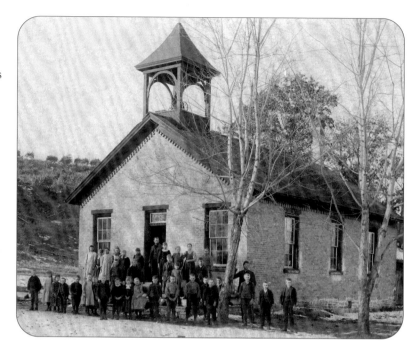

Three months after the St. Croix Valley Academy was organized, the Landes School (District 46), the ninth Afton school, was begun in Afton Township on May 7, 1868. Land for the school's site, which is now on 22nd Street about three-fourths mile west of Neal Avenue, was donated by a Mr. Fisher and Peter Landes. Its first board was comprised of Peter Landes, Benjamin Munson, and E.A. Rutherford. Measuring twenty-four by thirty-two feet, the schoolhouse was built for $1001.

For many years, George and Amanda Ellmann, who farmed the land across the road, supplied the school with water from their well. Some of the teachers also roomed with them, and in time, District 46 became known as the "Ellmann School." Bernice Ellmann Stoltzmann, the Ellmanns' daughter, remembered that the first teacher was Sophia Tyler, followed by Esther Hedstrom Schroeder, Mabel Myrhe, Lucille Dorgan Vitalis, Adeline Pauley, Edith Dahlgren, and Grace Rosenquist Nelson.

Next in the progression of Afton Village schools after the 1868 academy comes the historic brick school constructed in 1876, at a cost of six hundred dollars. When enrollment swelled to more than eighty pupils, many of whom came from the Swede Hill area, trustees leased a former grocery store building just north of the present Afton House Inn for the primary children. Their teacher was Miss May Person.

The eleventh school, Pennington, or District 65, started in the late 1870s or early 1880s. Land for the one-room Pennington School was apparently given or sold to the board by Charles and Mary Pennington who owned an eighty-acre farm nearby. This is the same engaging Mary Lange Pennington who ran the Afton Hotel.

A graduation souvenir from the year 1899/1900 lists George Pennington, director; August Anderson, treasurer; Albert Stone, clerk; and Florence E. Dick, teacher. Other teachers were Rose Ourada Hendrickson, Emma B. Esty, and Babette Johnson Robb. From Mrs. Robb's time in the 1950s, we have a printed folder for a Christmas program given by her students in the Afton Village Hall entitled "The Obliging Clock."

Rose Ourada Hendrickson revealed that her Depression-era salary between 1935 and 1938 ranged from $540 to $630 annually. Some of the family names from the Pennington district were Borene, Anderson, Groth, Nelson, Clymer, Jacobson, Korth, Schaeffer, Spadino, and Murphy. The Pennington school's life support system in later years was the Lincoln Nelson farm located across the road. Mr. Nelson served on the school board, and he and his wife provided room and board for grateful teachers in their home.

Afton's twelfth school was built for Swede Hill settlers in 1884 on 50th Street. Babette Johnson Robb taught at this school in the late 1940s. (Later, in 1970 while at the Bayport School, Mrs. Robb was a finalist in the Minnesota Teacher of the Year competition.) Swede Hill family names appearing on the rolls include Berglund, Granberg, Van Alstine, Beedle, Swanson, Stenstrom, Bondeson, Johnson, Benson, Peterson, Young, and Siebolds.

In 1950 all of the little Afton schools were gathered into one large District 22 blending city and country. As Washington County's last county superintendent of schools, legendary educator Grace McAlpine ably steered the few remaining schools under her direction through the traumatic process of consolidation at the century's midpoint. The loss of the little, old schools was deeply felt in most of the rural areas where the same families had attended and learned in these one-room buildings for as long as one hundred forty years.

The new Afton-Lakeland School opened in January 1952. Five years later, District 22 merged with the newly formed Stillwater School District 834, comprising the Withrow, Marine, Afton-Lakeland, Lake Elmo, Bayport, and Stillwater schools. And it is thus that the twelve different Afton schools have lost their pasts in the new, modern educational institutions to the north.

Public School Souvenir

1915

Our greatest glory is not in never failing But in rising every time we fail

SOUVENIR BOOKLET GIVEN TO SWEDE HILL SCHOOL SCHOLARS AT THE END OF THE TERM IN 1915. THERE WERE TWENTY-ONE STUDENTS THAT YEAR. THEIR TEACHER WAS ALICE G. NELSON.

FAITH OF
THEIR FATHERS

T he early Afton settlers, Yankees, Swedes, Germans alike, brought with them the "faith of their fathers." Their goal was to start churches, which they called "heaven's outlying colonies." They first met in homes and then built five churches here. Due to inevitable changes, however, Afton is now left with only two of them: St. Peter Lutheran Church on Neal Avenue and Memorial Lutheran Church on Highway 95 above the village.

Esther C. Robb's 1954 *History of the Afton Methodist Church* tells the story of the first attempts to bring organized religion to the area by circuit-riding Methodists. Taking root at Mounds Prairie near the old Afton-Woodbury Township line, Swedish Methodism organized a church in 1854. The first pastor was Rev. C.F. Forsberg. Called the "Townline" or "Mounds Prairie Church," it served parishioners for sixty years.

Then, because of deaths and removals, the Townline Church was abandoned about 1914. Only its small cemetery remains. One group within the church had become dissatisfied and built their own Swedish Methodist-Episcopal Church in Afton on land purchased in 1880 from Meredith and Harriet Thomas for fifty dollars. The new church opened in 1886 with Rev. L. Dahlgren as pastor. In 1893 a parsonage was built next door to the church on the east side. The parsonage has been moved to St. Croix Trail South and added onto, but the church remains at the same location, having been converted to a home.

While the Swedish Methodists were thus getting a good start, another group calling themselves "American Methodists" were renting and holding services in the American Church just down the street, a church that had been organized by the Congregationalists. This is the building that now houses the Afton Historical Museum.

For a short time beginning in August 1890, the American Methodists also rented part-time the new Swedish Methodist-Episcopal Church. By 1914, however, the two small, struggling Methodist congregations were united in the Minnesota Conference and

CONFIRMATION CLASS, SWEDISH EVANGELICAL LUTHERAN CHURCH, JUNE 24, 1911. BACK ROW: BERTIE JOHNSON, ERVIN PETERSON, EDWIN YOUNG, ARCHIE NELSON, ALFRED WALDIN, GODFREY NELSON. MIDDLE ROW: FRANK NELSON, ETHEL HEDSTROM, CLARA JOHNSON, HENNING SWANSON, SELMA HEDSTROM, EMMA NELSON, ROY JOHNSON, EMMA HEDSTROM, HILMA HERTZMAN, ELMER PETERSON. FRONT ROW: RAYMOND HENDRICKSON, MABEL NELSON, EDLA HENDRICKSON, REV. J. LUNDQUIST, FRANCES PETERSON, LAVINA LOFGREN, ALBERT PAULSON.

shared the use of the Swedish Church building.

But then there was the problem of which language to use—English or Swedish—the same old argument common among immigrant church factions. At first, an agreement to hold half the services in Swedish worked well enough, for Rev. J.P. Norton was skilled in both languages. After Norton left, however, the Conference was unable to provide another bilingual preacher. Swedish preachers had to be brought in by train, and sermons in Swedish were reduced to one per month. Feeling entitled to hear sermons in their beloved mother tongue, the Swedish parishioners were especially unhappy, while the American Methodists resented listening to even one sermon each month in Swedish.

Finally in 1919 the American faction gave up and returned to their first place of worship in the Congregational building, but by 1925 or so, according to Mrs. Robb's history, under the pastorate of Rev. W. Brown, the Methodists realized that the "discord between the Methodist Christians was an unholy thing." Merging once again with their Swedish brethren, the American Methodists carried their chairs out of the former Congregational building and up the street the few steps to the Methodist church.

Ultimately, in 1967 the Afton Methodist Church under the pastorate of Rev. Robert V. Laidig merged with the Lakeland United Church of Christ to build the new St. Croix Valley United Methodist Church in Lakeland. This large, modern structure was built and dedicated in 1969 on land donated by long-time Church of Christ members Phillip and Alta Carlson. When the size of this building was doubled later under the pastorate of Rev. Ray Boehlke, it was a dream come true for the two congregations.

The second Afton church, St. Peter Lutheran, was established on December 27, 1863, by German Missouri Synod Lutheran settlers from Martinsville, New York. Some of the first parishioners were Michael and August Stegemann, Fred Markgraf, and the widow Mrs. Pagel and her children. Services were at first held in homes, usually by Pastor E. Rolf of St. Paul.

In 1865 three acres of land for a church site and cemetery was purchased from Christian Pagel for $22.50. Lumber for the first church came from an abandoned sawmill that was dismantled in Lakeland. The first pastor was Rev. J. Karrer. In 1868 Pastor Ottomar Cloeter, who had been ministering to the Ojibwa Indians in northern Minnesota for ten years, arrived to serve the church for twenty-nine years. A log schoolhouse was built on the north side of the church in 1872; a Mr. Koenig was the first teacher.

This steadfast congregation continued to grow, and in January 1898, built a new wooden church which was destroyed when it was struck by lightning in August 1924. A new brick church was erected for twenty thousand dollars and dedicated on July 19, 1925.

During the pastorate of Rev. Ernest Kanning from 1964 to 1970, St. Peter's constructed a parish building for church classes and a pastor's office. A new parish hall opened in 1971, and the next year, a nursery school for four-year-olds. And in the 1990s the fervor and tenacity of St. Peter's members for all these years continues to bear luxuriant, spiritual fruit. The church's many organizations include Ladies Aid, youth and young adult groups, and junior and senior choirs.

Another group of worshipers, the Congregationalists, organized a church in Afton on June 24, 1858; led by Rev. Simon Putnam, the denomination claimed thirteen members. For ten years this brave but dwindling flock met in either homes or in the schoolhouse. Pastor Putnam built the present "little red house" as his parsonage in 1859, and the Congregationalist church on Washington Street was completed in September 1868. This was the church later used by the American Methodists who eventually purchased the building; when the American Methodists later merged with the Swedish Methodists, the church building was

WALTER AND JOAN MONDALE ON ELECTION DAY, 1976. FOR A TIME, VICE PRESIDENT MONDALE CLAIMED SWEDE HILL IN SOUTHEAST AFTON AS HIS LEGAL RESIDENCE; THE RESIDENCE ACTUALLY BELONGED TO JOAN'S PARENTS, THE MAXWELL ADAMSES.

sold to several men's groups including the Modern Woodmen of America. Ultimately, probably in the late 1920s, the Afton bank foreclosed the mortgage it held on the property, and the building was purchased by the village for six hundred dollars.

In its secular guise, the former Congregationalist/Methodist church became a meeting place for various organizations, council chambers, election polling place, public forum, and dance hall. About the time it ceased to be a house of worship, it was moved one lot south and a basement excavated. Giving Afton the nearest thing to a theatre, a stage was added, where many a melodramatic play has been presented by community and church groups. One such play in the 1930s was entitled "Yimmy Yohnson's Yob." In more recent years the stage has accommodated a number of old-fashioned Chautauquas sponsored by the Afton Historical Society.

National media attention focused on the old building in 1976, when Senator Walter F. Mondale, then a legal resident of Afton, voted there on his way to becoming vice president of the United States.

Unlike their German brethren, the Swedish Lutherans made a faltering start in Afton. Eager to preserve their religious heritage from Sweden, they at first met in members' homes, the Landes schoolhouse, and a one-room church with kerosene lanterns. The first would-be organizers in 1861 were Peter T. Peterson and

John C. Picullel, but this early attempt to establish a Swedish Lutheran Church in Afton failed, and many Swedes moved to Vasa or Red Wing where Lutheran churches were already well rooted.

The present Memorial Lutheran Church, originally called the Swedish Evangelical Lutheran Church, dates to 1882 and owes its beginnings in large part to Carl Swanlund from Sweden who arrived in Valley Creek in 1881. Swanlund opened his home for meetings and in other ways nurtured the fledgling congregation. The Lutherans called him "the prime moving spirit" in the formation of their church.

The "founding meeting" convened in the home of John and Sessla Lofgren, which was located north of where Highway 95 swings south at the top of the hill in Afton. The Lofgrens had come on different voyages from Sweden directly to Afton in 1869. At this meeting, the fourteen founding families decided to construct a small frame building twenty-four by thirty-six feet by twelve feet high. Mrs. Lofgren chose the scenic site next to Evergreen Cemetery. The simple little structure costing eight hundred dollars was dedicated in October 1882. A village landmark, it has ever since been called "the little white church on the hill."

Starting with Rev. A.F. Tornell, twenty-one pastors have ministered to the spiritual needs of this congregation. Rev. Carl W. Almen served the church through the longest and undoubtedly the most stressful pastorate, which included the Great Depression, World War II, and the beginning of the Cold War. He was a big, powerful but gentle man who resembled the Youngdahl brothers, Luther and Reuben, who became prominent in the political and religious life of Minnesota. For seventeen years Rev. Almen steered the church through many changes including the 1932 refurbishing and the addition of a basement and an eighteen-foot extension of the building to the north.

Because the 1932 renovation was paid for largely through memorial gifts, Pastor Almen suggested changing the church's name to "Memorial Lutheran Church." Oddly, this change was never officially adopted by the congregation but just simply evolved over the next few years.

Following in Pastor Almen's footsteps, succeeding pastors lived up to his high level of leadership. Under Rev. Roger C. Mackey in the 1960s, an attractive parsonage and a large fellowship hall that offers a breathtaking vista of the St. Croix River were completed. In 1991 under the able direction of Pastor Marvin L. Larson, the congregation built a new church, which was completed in time for Christmas Eve services.

Fortunately for posterity, the Swedish Lutherans obliged historians by publishing two excellent histories, one upon the fiftieth anniversary of the church, and the other upon its centennial. Their communal sense of history has also so far preserved their pioneer church. To date, Memorial members have not been able to face the thought of

INTERIOR AND EXTERIOR VIEWS OF THE PLAIN-FACED ST. PAULUS GERMAN LUTHERAN CHURCH THAT STOOD AT THE NORTH END OF AFTON. THE CHURCH IS LONG GONE, BUT THE ST. PAULUS PARSONAGE, SEEN ON THE RIGHT IN THE BOTTOM PHOTO, IS STILL EXTANT. IT IS NOW A PRIVATE RESIDENCE.

razing their beloved little white church on the hill; it remains there still, uneasily awaiting its fate.

The fifth Afton church, St. Paulus German Lutheran Church, stood one block north of the St. Croix Valley Academy, where County 21 and Highway 95 fork. Like the Mounds Prairie Methodist Church, St. Paulus has departed, leaving behind a small cemetery. The church's little gray parsonage on St. Croix Trail at the north end of the village is also extant, giving quiet testimony to the pastor who lived within its walls and preached in the church next door.

Several people who were baptized and confirmed in the German Lutheran Church are still alive, but their memories for specific details have grown vague. All that is left of this old institution are a few pictures, a few names, and a few anecdotes.

One former member said she believed a prominent official of the church, Alfred Lambrecht, rather than risk losing its records, simply took them home when the church closed. The results are the same: we have no written record of the congregation's life and accomplishments. Think of our excitement if someone from the old village should unexpectedly discover this cache.

Ruby Spreeman Henning remembers that the men invariably sat on the right side of the German Lutheran church—the side of "honor"—while the women and children were relegated to the left or side of less importance.

Another member of the Spreeman family by marriage recalled a preacher who usually showed up for services with a quart of whiskey in his pocket. "Once he hurt his leg hopping off the train," she said, "and of course everyone could guess how the accident had probably happened. Some of those sermons grew quite interesting."

For many years, Ferdinand Richert pumped and played the reed organ. Mr. Richert once taught at the St. Croix Valley Academy and ran one of Afton's oldest general stores on Washington Street (a two-story frame building across from the present post office that eventually collapsed under a heavy burden of snow in the late 1970s). Succeeding Richert at the organ was Mabel Zollner Weyer. According to her daughter, Elvina Zollner Mueller of Lakeland, "Mother had very little musical training, so it was a really hard job for her. But she thought it was her duty."

Both Elvina Mueller and Ella Johnson remember that the services were always in German. "We didn't have the slightest idea about what was going on," they agreed.

That old German Lutheran Church, which long kept the faith of its members green, has been gone now for about fifty years. Its ignoble end was to become lost as part of a chicken house in Afton. If the town cares enough for its ancestors asleep in the forlorn little cemetery to give it the attention it deserves, then the demise of the forgotten church will not seem quite so sad.

WHERE FOREFATHERS SLEEP

Three cemeteries served old Afton Village: Evergreen Community, Swedish Evangelical Lutheran, and St. Paulus Lutheran. Lying outside the village limits but within the old Afton Township were four others: the Fahlstrom cemetery, Mount Hope, Rice-Landes, and St. Peter Lutheran.

Outlining the beginnings of Evergreen Community Cemetery, historian Edward D. Neill wrote, "At the time of the platting of the Village of Afton, the proprietors set apart and donated to the village twenty acres in section twenty-two for a cemetery. It was dedicated in 1855. This property was not actually deeded to the Evergreen Cemetery Association until May 28, 1873, when it became the legal owner."

Organized under a constitution and by-laws, Evergreen manages its property and graves through the Evergreen Cemetery Association Board, which consists of a sexton and nine trustees. The present sexton, Floyd Hallquist, a grandson of Afton pioneer Elof Hallquist, cuts the grass, oversees burials, and directs workdays scheduled by the board. Trustees of this beautiful cemetery include David Berglund, David Robb, Ed Robb, David Haslund, Jon Johnson, Tom Johnson, Beverley Lloyd, Margaret Lonergan, Wesley Sanderson, and Kerry White.

Visitors often remark on the misshapen Norway spruce tree just inside the gates. In 1882, to mark the completion of the Swedish Evangelical Lutheran Church, Sessla Lofgren planted two Norway spruce seedlings there. These seedlings were likely grown from cones the immigrants brought to America since the tree is not indigenous to this country. Both trees grew and flourished until struck by lightning, which destroyed one and gave the other its peculiar, flattened-out top.

Despite its odd appearance, the surviving Norway was declared state champion by the Department of Natural Resources in June 1981. Measured the next year, the church's centennial, the tree was sixty-three feet tall, spreading seventy-two feet at its crown; its

FUNERAL AT ST. PAULUS GERMAN LUTHERAN CHURCH.

51

trunk was 132.5 inches in circumference. Sessla Lofgren's needled symbol of thanks to God so long ago has apparently pleased Him.

What most people do not know is that there are actually two cemeteries surrounding the original Swedish Evangelical Lutheran Church (now Memorial Lutheran)—Evergreen and the Lutheran cemetery. The earliest burial date we can find in the Lutheran section is 1884. In 1892, Christine Roen tells us in *A Goodly Heritage*, her centennial history of Memorial Lutheran Church, the congregation bought a small lot east of the church from Evergreen Cemetery for ten dollars. More space was added to the Lutheran cemetery in 1938, when the church acquired some tax-forfeited property by paying the back taxes. William Lofgren, son of John and Sessla Lofgren, bought the lots at a

sheriff's sale, and he and Enoch Swanson assumed supervision of that cemetery. Mathilda Swanson, Enoch's mother, contributed to a perpetual care fund which is still active today. Wesley Sanderson is the present caretaker of the Lutheran cemetery in addition to serving as trustee on the Evergreen Cemetery Board.

The St. Paulus German Lutheran Cemetery, abandoned in 1942, has been without official care for nearly sixty years. For many years, Gust and Albert Spreeman, who had family buried there, valiantly fought back nature's encroachment, mowing the grass and eradicating the poison ivy, but both of them have now passed on. In more recent years, Ronald Rosenquist has worked to maintain the cemetery. His boyhood home was the former parsonage.

One cheerful ray of light pierced this dismal cloud in 1989 when Boy Scout Chris Westmoreland from the Memorial Lutheran Church troop adopted St. Paulus Cemetery as his Eagle Scout project. He and his fellow scouts raised and straightened some of the sunken markers, weeded the grounds, cut the grass, planted day lilies, and constructed a handsome new "St. Paulus Cemetery" sign, a luxury the old cemetery enjoyed for the first time.

St. Paulus monuments and markers range from imposing and ornate to small and delicate. One tiny white stone, still upright despite its frail look, is heartbreakingly pathetic. Its simple message: "Pohl, born and died 1905. Asleep in Jesus." Another stone that appears to have been hand-chiseled reads: "Daughter of H. Spreeman born, died, July 8, 1906." The German names found in this cemetery include Albrecht, Boenning, Frederick,

Gedatus, Heuer, Sassa, Schuster, Trebus, Zabel, and Zollner.

The smallest Afton cemetery is the one usually referred to as "the Indian cemetery," the resting place of celebrated missionary Jacob Fahlstrom, his Ojibwa wife Margaret Bungo Fahlstrom, and some of their children. Because the Fahlstrom log cabin and burial ground are now private property, its location will remain undisclosed. I searched for it alone and as unobtrusively as possible on three different days. Pushing through tangled buckthorn and brush, I was about to give up the search when, climbing a gentle hill, all at once I spied several crosses and monuments in a small clearing, illuminated by the bright August sun. Made from granite, metal, and concrete, the Fahlstrom markers are surprisingly intact. One steel cross bears a tiny, delicate image of the crucified Christ.

Peering at this odd collection of gravestones with their ancient and eroding figures, and remembering that this amazing man lived right here in Afton, I sensed the irony of our best known pioneer's lying in such a small, secret, and well-hidden cemetery.

THIS CRUCIFIX MARKER IN THE FAHLSTROM CEMETERY IS HANDMADE FROM METAL PIPE.

On September 6, 1964, the Historical Society of the Minnesota Conference of the Methodist Church dedicated a memorial marker on the graves of Jacob and Margaret Fahlstrom. Perhaps eighty people climbed to the top of the hill by a path then more accessible to honor Minnesota's first Swede. More than forty Fahlstrom descendants came from as far away as Manhattan, Kansas.

Mount Hope, Afton's oldest cemetery, is so close to extinction that soon we may be only reading about it. Reposing high on the big hill just above the old village, Mount Hope occupies lot 17 west of County Highway 21 and south of State Highway 95. It was officially assigned five acres but never grew beyond a stingy one-half acre. The gravesites lie on the hill so far above the highways that vandals must have felt safely invisible in their nasty desecration.

According to Alvin Hedstrom, the first burials took place at Mount Hope in 1854 and the last in 1892. In a 1952 newspaper article, he noted that the cemetery had been sadly neglected for at least forty years, and called this a "rebuke to the community."

Mount Hope was dedicated the same year the village was platted, in 1855. Clearly, Afton's founding fathers were men of large, generous natures, for the men who did the actual platting—R. Haskell, Joseph Haskell, H.L. Thomas, and Charles S. Getchell—also donated the land for Mount Hope. Of these, only Charles Getchell is buried in Mount Hope. Alongside him is his wife, Electa Getchell, who died at the age of thirty-two in 1857. Electa, a poet at heart, named both Afton and Mount Hope Cemetery.

Four Civil War veterans are buried in Mount Hope, including Rev. Simon Putnam and his son Myron, both of whom were casualties of the war. Young Myron Putnam was sixteen when he enlisted in the Union Army as a musician; wounded in service, he died at eighteen in 1863. Rev. Simon Putnam was chaplain in the Third Regiment, Minnesota Volunteers; returning home to Afton ill in 1864, he died a few days later at age forty-two. Putnam had been the first preacher of any denomination to organize religion in the village, and the first school superintendent. This conscientious pioneer taught village young people in the kitchen of his home, the Congregationalist parsonage, which today is the "little red house."

The other Civil War veterans at Mount Hope are Charles C. Cushing, reportedly a man of great character, who built Afton's second hotel in 1867 (much remodeled, this hotel is now the Afton House Inn); and Isaac Van Vleck, who was discharged from a hospital in June 1865 and died fifteen years later in Afton.

Patriotism was rampant in early Afton, and come Decoration Day (now Memorial Day), schoolboys from the little brick schoolhouse under the direction of Yankee school board member Richard Buswell each year marched up the steep hill to Mount Hope and decorated the graves of the Civil War veterans. Ray Pennington, son of Charles Pennington, carried the flag. Urging some of the straggling youngsters into the line of march, Mr. Buswell would tell them, "You too may some day have to go to war." Some of these same boys did have to fight in World War I.

Benjamin Babcock, Afton's physician for a decade beginning in 1860 is also buried at Mount Hope, and his is a particularly poignant story. Babcock and his wife Amelia buried two children there in 1862 and 1870. Then Babcock himself, only thirty-four years old, also died in 1870 and is buried beside his children. In 1882 Amelia Babcock sold land for thirty dollars to the organizers of the Swedish Evangelical Church, later to be called Memorial Lutheran.

Another civilian of special interest in Mount Hope is Samuel H. Paterson (also spelled Patterson), who in 1856 built Afton's first hotel, a twenty-four by twenty-four foot structure that burned in 1861. Other names in this pathetic little cemetery include Guernsey, McDonald, Mitchell, Owen, Palmer, and Stouffer. We are indebted to the late Oliver Charley for recording these names, because official records are nonexistent.

It is not accurate to say that Afton has generally cared nothing about Mount Hope Cemetery. Various community groups have struggled sporadically to rescue it from vandalism and oblivion. Working with the most heart have been the 4-H club, the Boy Scouts, church youth groups, the Washington County Historical Society, and the Afton Historical Society.

The Briggs family, early berry farmers on the bluff below Mount Hope and owning land adjacent to the cemetery, did their best to keep nature from reclaiming the old burial ground. First came George and Sarah Briggs, then Harold "Jerry" and Hazel Briggs to mow and rake. Today, the Briggses are gone, but one neighbor to the cemetery, Bill Isaacson, an airline pilot, cuts the grass as if it were his own land.

A fifth pioneer cemetery, the Rice-Landes or Mounds Prairie Cemetery stands at the southeast corner of the intersection of County Highway 15 (Manning Avenue) and 22nd Street or Valley Creek Road. The Rice-Landes name derives from two prominent pioneer families buried there. Its other designation remembers the little Mounds Prairie Church built at one corner of the lot in 1853 or 1854. This church was the Swedes' first humble attempt to establish a house of worship in Afton. Its work long since taken over by the Swedish Methodist-Episcopal Church in Afton Village, the pre-Civil War structure was finally dismantled in the mid-1940s by farmer Harry Rice. All that is left today is the small but immaculately groomed burial ground.

The earliest known burial in the Rice-Landes cemetery is that of Fannie Guy who died in 1859 at the age of four. Another burial of note was that of Charles G. Holmes in 1913. Holmes, along with Mons Johnson and Rev. C.F. Forsberg, was a major force in organizing the Mounds Prairie Church.

The St. Peter Lutheran Cemetery is located just behind the church on Neal Avenue; rows of handsome old cedars and spruces define the burial ground. The first burial in St. Peter Cemetery was that of a child, Theodore Kumm, son of August Kumm and his wife Caroline, nee Bahnemann, born September 5, 1865, and buried less than a year later on June 14, 1866.

For most of its existence St. Peter's Cemetery has been assiduously tended by members of the congregation, volunteering or elected to the task. In the 1960s and 1970s, young people through the Afton Arrows 4-H Club made care of the cemetery their own mission. Today a committee of Earl Mueller, Ferd Stoltzmann, and David Hauck shoulders responsibility for this demanding work.

But whether carefully tended on a systematic basis or woefully neglected in sad indifference, all of Afton's seven cemeteries possess certain characteristics not found in larger urban cemeteries. Perhaps it is merely the rural surroundings, the birdsong, the open land, the smell of earth after the plow has cut deep. We may not be able to describe it, but we all recognize it. The atmosphere of our Afton cemeteries is aptly captured in Thomas Gray's well-known "Elegy written in a Country Churchyard":

THE BROKEN BERRY FAMILY MONUMENT IN MOUNT HOPE CEMETERY. DAVID AND ELIZABETH BERRY CAME TO AFTON FROM ENGLAND IN 1854 AND RAISED FOUR CHILDREN HERE.

> *Beneath the rugged elms, that yew-tree's shade,*
> *Where heaves the earth in many a molding heap,*
> *Each in his narrow cell for ever laid,*
> *The rude forefathers of the hamlet sleep.*

EARLY
BUSINESSES

A fton was once a beehive of about fifteen retail businesses. Villagers usually stayed home and bought their goods and services here rather than make the long trip to "the cities." Cars were scarce and uncertain of performance. Until 1926, old Highway 12 from the Twin Cities was only a gravel road. When Aftonites were "doctoring," as they said, and needed medical trips to Stillwater, Hudson, or St. Paul, many of them hitched rides with generous neighbors.

Old Afton contained an abundance of general stores with both groceries and hardware under the same roof. Also in good supply were blacksmith shops. Blacksmiths like the Bolles family in Valley Creek, and Andrew Sjoholm and Chris Christensen in Afton often not only shoed horses but also manufactured farm equipment and wagons.

OPPOSITE: THE BENJAMIN PELHAM SQUIRES HOUSE, BUILT IN 1876. LEFT TO RIGHT: UNIDENTIFIED WOMAN, RACHEL SQUIRES (PEABODY), EMMA ROSENQUIST SQUIRES, FRANK SQUIRES, AND FRANCES SQUIRES (MORTON) IN BUGGY.

AFTON BLACKSMITH CHRIS CHRISTENSEN HAD HIS SHOP ON WASHINGTON STREET, JUST NORTH OF SELMA'S ICE CREAM PARLOR. THIS PHOTO WAS TAKEN JANUARY 9, 1932.

One of the best-remembered general stores was the Richert-Peterson-Pothen store on the west side of Washington Street. This historic building collapsed under the weight of a massive snow blanket in the late 1970s, and Squire House Gardens next door has recently acquired the site for a sunken garden.

The abstract for this property on lots five and six of block 17 dates to November 13, 1883, when it was transferred from Leavitt and Rhoda Olds to Aaron Harper and Abram Gillespie, who may have been the first retailers on this site. In fact, Durand Rotzel, who with his wife Charlotte purchased the old store in 1976, was so sure of this that he painted a sign reading "HARPER AND GILLESPIE" and attached it to the old building for the Bicentennial Fourth of July parade that year.

This claim is disputed, however, by Afton resident Harvey Richert, who asserts that his grandfather, Ferdinand H. Richert purchased the property in 1897, constructed the building, and conducted the first trade in it. During part of the time he owned the store, Richert rented it to Albert Stone who kept a stock of buggies stored in the attic. There was a ramp on the south side of the building down which the buggies were rolled as customers came to buy them.

In September 1926, Ferdinand sold the store to his son, Frederick E. Richert. He and his children, Henry "Heinie", Harvey, and Catherine, took turns minding the store. This old German family exhibited a progressiveness ahead of their time by buying a large Ford truck and picking up their fresh produce in St. Paul three times a week.

After World War II, Hiram "Reek" Peterson, who helped organize Afton's fire department, and his wife, Marian Clymer Peterson, took charge of the store in 1948. Marian was later Afton's postmistress and kept her office in a corner of the store, which she and Hiram ran devotedly until his death in 1963. Afterwards, Henry "Hank" and Gladys Pothen rented the business, moving their own grocery trade across the street from the bank building where they had run a competing business. A volunteer fireman like Peterson, Hank Pothen was the first chief of the Lake St. Croix Beach Fire Department.

Across the street and a little south of the site of the old Richert-Peterson-Pothen store, Selma's Ice Cream Parlor is an Afton landmark. Now thriving under Laine McGee's artistry with all her added print,

FERDINAND H. RICHERT AND HIS WIFE MARTHA LIVED IN THE TWO-STORY FRAME HOUSE NEXT DOOR TO THE NORTH OF THEIR STORE.

trophy, and entertainment features, it would amaze little, white-haired Selma Swanson Holberg were she to step into her old shop today.

The original small frame structure was built as a dwelling by the Holberg family about 1880. Some fifty years later, descendants Eddie Holberg, Selma's husband, and his brother Herbert opened their home as a confectionery with a pool table and a piano in the living room. The attached structure on the north, now part of Laine McGee's enlarged establishment, was originally built to serve as a grocery store; later it housed a fish bait shop, and then the Afton Post Office following World War II. Afton natives who represented Uncle Sam there included George "Judd" Eastwood, Bill Broecker, and Rachel Squires Peabody. Rachel's grandfather, Benjamin Squires, had been one of the earliest postmasters in South Afton. (Located down the River Road about a mile south of present Afton, South Afton centered roughly where the Dick Herreid home now stands at 4524 River Road; it once had a store, grain elevator, sawmill, and lumber yard.)

Perhaps Selma's and Eddie's biggest triumph was their custom of serving midnight chicken dinners to the crowd from the nearby Wolf dance hall. That hall stood on the boulevard of Washington Street just north of Frank Spreeman, Jr.'s house, which is extant at 35th Street and St. Croix Trail. (Earlier occupants of this house had been Afton pioneers Fred and Ida Johnson, the parents of flyer Roy Johnson.)

After Eddie Holberg died in 1936, Selma managed the business alone for another thirty years. Her life at the parlor spanned more than fifty years. Staying flexible with the economy of the times, she switched capably from ice cream parlor to cafe (sandwiches only), to tavern (beer only), and even to casino. Slot machines enjoyed some popularity until Governor Luther Youngdahl outlawed them in the 1940s.

SELMA SWANSON AS A YOUNG GIRL WITH HER BROTHER MANFRED AND SISTER ESTHER (PETERSON). SELMA'S PARENTS EMIGRATED FROM SWEDEN IN 1868 AND SETTLED IN WELCH, MINNESOTA. IN 1911 THEY MOVED TO A BERRY FARM WEST OF AFTON AND JOINED THE MEMORIAL LUTHERAN CHURCH. THE FAMILY INCLUDED TWO SONS AND SIX DAUGHTERS.

Although Selma's experience with people was mostly happy, she recalled a big exception. After Eddie died, a car with four fishermen broke through the ice on the river. Two of the men drowned, and the other two were brought into her place. "They dried their wet clothes by my pot-bellied stove, and I gave them my husband's clothes to wear. Steam covered everything and made the wallpaper peel. I lost a day's business caring for them. They left and never returned the clothes or got in touch with me," Selma said sadly.

Selma's vigor was already beginning to fade when the St. Croix River swept almost over the parlor's roof during the great flood of 1965. Today, painted near the top of the porch is a little sign, 1965 FLOOD, with blue wave lines to show the high water mark. During this flood, as if in response to the calamity, Selma was confined to the hospital.

Coming to Selma's rescue, Afton resident Elmer H. Smith, who invented the acetylene torch and founded the Smith Welding Company (TESCOM), sized up her predicament and paid the cost of resuscitating her structure after its long immersion in water. Acknowledging his help, Selma wrote on a small scrap of stationery:

> Dear friends Mr. and Mrs. Smith:
> I cannot find words to express my gratitude to you for the help you extended me in putting my place in order after the flood disaster. When I came home from the hospital, all looked impossible—my heart went weak—then you called and said you would help.
> It was a wonderful message as I am only an insignificant person. I wish there was something I might do for you in some small way to let you know what it means to me to have so much kindness offered. I will say the world is a better place in which to live because of you. Therefore I will say thank you! And thanks again.
> > With much love,
> > Selma

Selma Swanson Holberg died in 1966. Prominent in the Afton Historical Museum is a display case with remnants of this little Swedish woman's life: her wedding gown and shoes, her wedding certificate, two photographs, and one of Selma's trusty ice cream scoops.

A third Afton business, the Afton Barber Shop, is a fledgling compared to the old store and Selma's, but historic nonetheless. Afton had no barber until Herbert Sill moved here about 1915 from Hastings, Minnesota. Born in 1884 in Park Rapids, Minnesota, Herb had married Clara Schultz and homesteaded for a few years with his

bride in Saskatchewan, Canada, where they lived in a log cabin with sod roof and engaged in wheat farming with a pair of oxen.

Deciding this venture in that northern outpost would not pay off, the Sills returned to Minnesota and set up housekeeping in Hastings. There Herb learned barbering through the apprentice system (there were no barber schools then). When the man he worked for one day suggested: "Afton is a nice, little town north of here. Why don't you go up there and open a shop?" Herbert did just that.

After setting up his first chair in the Afton Hotel, owned and run by Mary Pennington, he next moved his trade across the street to the basement of the brick bank building. When it became apparent that he could make a living barbering, he bought a little square frame building, formerly a bachelor's quarters that stood behind the George Slater house on the corner of St. Croix Trail and Upper 34th Street. Moving it to Washington Street, where it shoulders up against the larger Lerk's Bar, he added the square, front facade to the pint-sized structure and began his long-surviving business.

At the rear of the shop, behind a plasterboard partition with a door, Herb installed an old-time four-legged, white bathtub. In addition to haircuts (which cost twenty-five cents compared to nine dollars today), he also provided Saturday night baths. Remember that Afton was then mainly an agricultural rather than a bedroom community and that Saturday night marked the happy climax of the week. Farmers flocked into Afton to visit, shop, drink, wash, and be shorn. Emerging from the dusty fields at sundown, they especially relished the lure of a store-bought bath.

The water for the baths had to be pumped by hand from a cistern to a fifty-gallon tank hung from the ceiling and heated by bottled gas. "As a boy, I was assigned the job of pumping that handle up and down to keep the tank full," remembered Herb's son Harold, clutching his back in mock pain.

On Friday and Saturday nights, when the customers bunched up much more than at other times, the old barber shop rang with warm, neighborly talk. Farmers compared notes on their ever-changing vocation and discussed endless details of village life. Along with the tavern, the barber shop filled an acute need to socialize in Afton. The row of little wire-backed chairs common to drugstores of the era was always filled on these two evenings.

In 1947, after thirty years of shearing heads, Herbert Sill retired, and Harold Sill took his father's place as Afton's barber. Making a few changes, Harold rigged up a communication system to expedite the flow of patrons. Because some of the men preferred to do their waiting next door in the bar, he wired a signal device between Lerk's and the barber shop. When the barber finished a haircut or shave, he reached up and pushed a button that activated a buzzer in the bar, signaling the next customer to step back into the barber shop. The buzzer is still on the east wall where you can see it if you look closely, but the "next-please" signal was disconnected years ago.

Harold cut hair and shaved his customers with a master's touch. Working at a deliberate pace, he made the sitting time fly by with the friendly, informed conversation his customers grew to expect. As a successful barber, he knew he

HERB AND CLARA SILL, JUNE 1944.

THE WOLF DANCE HALL (ALSO KNOWN AS THE WOLF COMMUNITY HALL OR AFTON AUDITORIUM HALL) STOOD BY THE CREEK AT THE SOUTH END OF THE VILLAGE ON THE WEST SIDE OF WASHINGTON STREET.

had to do more than just cut hair—he had to inform, soothe, and even entertain his customers as well. Harold just plain liked people and treated them well—another absolute requirement of an effective barber which this hometown barber fulfilled in Christian charity.

In the nearly eighty years the Afton Barber Shop has serviced area residents, it has had only four barbers—the gentlemen Sills, and two, smart little lady barbers. When Harold retired in 1978, Barbara Costa replaced him and renovated the midget building into a new and improved version of the old place while still preserving its historic look. After a year or so, Barb was succeeded by perky Peggy Knowling, who seems with her swift craftsmanship and warm banter to be headed, like the Sills, for long service.

STREETSCAPE WITH BARBER SHOP, LERK'S, AFTON CITIZENS' STATE BANK BUILDING, AND THE AFTON HOUSE INN.

THE BERGLUNDS: A SWEDISH SAGA

A s you wind your way up the coulee road at the south end of Afton, look to the right on one of the curves about halfway up. You'll spot a partial view of the Berglund house and barn. And if you have reason to drive up the long, blacktopped driveway, you will behold a restored farm worthy of any of the slick "house beautiful" magazines. David and Sandy Berglund have wrought a miracle of change in their family's old Oak Grove farm.

Before Dave and Sandy moved in, while bachelor uncles Fred and Herbert Berglund still lived there, folks viewed the place with a touch of compassion. Here was one more instance of old people, doomed by the times, trying to keep their home and independence. After Fred and Herbert died, when Dave and Sandy chose to move out of their modern home farther south and tackle the old homestead in 1984, some of their friends questioned their judgment. "It was a gigantic undertaking," said Sandy, "but the longer we worked on it, the more attached to the project we became."

Fred and Herbert's parents had come to Afton from Sweden. In the old country, their name had been simply "Berg." There the family fought a land inhospitable to farming and an economy allowing little beyond the basics. Between 1868 and 1871, the brothers' grandparents, patriarch Eric Gustaf Berg and his wife Lena ("Stina") Ehrenberg Berg saw three of their children—Christina, John, and Charles—leave their home in Kanna, Cronoberg, Smaland, Sweden, for America. Eric and Lena finally made the long ocean voyage with their youngest daughter Lizzie in 1879. Soon after their arrival, the family changed their name to Berglund.

John Berglund, a shoemaker, set up a shoe shop in Stillwater across the street from where the Lowell Inn now stands. Charles and Christina lived in Stillwater with their brother John who, having preceded them to America by three years, was therefore wiser in the ways of his adopted country. When Eric Gustaf, also a cobbler, arrived with Lena and Lizzie, they lived in the little blue house on the east side of Afton's main street at the south end of the village. Just north of the former Albert and Lydia Brown Swanson house, this blue house was later occupied by Tony Hedstrom.

In 1885 Charles Berglund, after trying shoemaking and lumbering, bought an eighty-acre farm from Erick Thompson in section 27 of Afton. This developed into the Oak Grove farm that is now Dave and Sandy's pride and joy. Charles's purchase included a simple house, a small barn, a dug well, and assorted sheds. The fourteen by eighteen-foot house consisted of one room, a small lean-to kitchen, and a loft. To this Charles added a shed at the rear as an improvement to the kitchen. The soil and terrain of Charles Berglund's farm resembled the farms in Sweden—rocky, hilly, and lacking a single level field in the whole acreage.

The year after buying the farm, Charles married Martha Benson, who had also emigrated from Sweden. The daughter of poor farmers in the old country, Martha had arrived in Minnesota in the spring of 1880 and taken a job as a nanny and housekeeper for the well-to-do Fairchilds on Summit Avenue in St. Paul. Martha's ability to speak English was sharpened by caring for the Fairchild children.

Martha's name in Sweden had been Matra (or "Marti") Bengtson (meaning son of Bengt). Her father Bengt Goransson and his wife Christina lost two of their children, John and Martha, to the "America fever" sweeping their nation in the late nineteenth century. A third Bengtson child, Charlotta, stayed in Sweden according to custom to care for her parents.

Fortunately for us and the Berglund family history, we have a vivid word picture of Martha Benson and her family in Sweden through almost two hundred remarkable letters, which the present generation of the family have had translated into English. Fear tinges all the parents' sad letters, a fear that they would never see those children again, a fear that became reality. Martha's brother John did many kinds of work, and his job as a miner in Wisconsin particularly alarmed his parents. Whenever his letters were delayed, they worried that he was an accident victim in the mines or had died in some other way.

The Benson letters also speak often of God, the crucifixion of Christ, religious anniversaries like Pentecost, and the necessity for faith on the part of these brave people. One wish expressed over and over was "We hope your health is good because that is God's greatest gift of all."

Bengt and Christina Goransson expected that their children would go to the United States only temporarily, make as much money as fast as possible, and then return to Sweden. Of course, most of the Swedish immigrants became permanent settlers. In one letter, Bengt Goransson laments, "It sounds as if Matra has changed her mind about returning to Sweden." In another, he remarks, "It is hard to be old and have your children in America."

One sad letter dated July 2, 1886, from Martha's father tells of her mother's death at age fifty-nine of the "death sickness," marked by severe coughing. Christina had hoped to one day be able to go to America to see her children, but that was not to be. Then on December 14, 1900, Charlotta wrote to Martha with the heartbreaking news that their father Bengt Goransson had passed away.

At the opposite end of the emotional scale, Charles Berglund once received a jubilant letter from his brother-in-law Fred Graff, a Minneapolis resident married to Lizzie Berglund, who had learned "the bar in Afton has been closed down." For the most

A LETTER FROM SWEDEN, MARTHA BENSON BERGLUND, 1930S.

part however, "the Benson letters make pretty grim reading," noted Dave Berglund.

Charles and Martha Berglund raised eight children at Oak Grove farm, six boys and two girls—Fred, Albert, Edwin, Elvera, Esther, Arthur, Emmett, and Herbert. All of them worked hard to make the farm prosper. At its peak, production on the Oak Grove farm reached an enviable level of variety and quality. Needing more acreage, Charles rented 150 acres from his legendary Swede Hill neighbor, Tom Cooney, and purchased additional land until the Berglund parcel totaled some 270 acres—enough to support the variety and volume achieved by the family.

At one time or another the Oak Grove operation included almost every kind of farming possible: a dairy herd with blood lines carefully developed over the years; poultry with as many as 660 eggs incubated in the spring; Perchean work horses selected and bred; and prize-winning crops improved with each new season. Keeping abreast of the times, the Berglunds sowed the newest strains of seeds and won Washington County grain competition awards for their winter wheat, oats, rye, buckwheat, timothy seed, and white navy beans. In December 1914, the Berglund farm won second place overall at the Stillwater Mid-Winter Fair. The next year, at the Minnesota State Fair, their corn took the grand sweepstakes.

In connection with their extensive apple orchard, the Berglunds tended beehives and harvested honey. As nearly all farmers did then, they also raised and marketed garden produce. In a taped interview conducted by his nephew Harold Berglund in 1985, Fred Berglund, who died later that year at the age of ninety-seven, described the way the brothers hauled their vegetables and fruit to the St. Paul market. They loaded the horse-drawn wagon and left the farm at 1:00 a.m. to make sure they arrived in the city by daylight.

Oak Grove farm also gained a reputation for its seven acres of onions. Labor intensive, the onions required painstaking weeding done on hands and knees with short-handled hoes. As the plants grew taller, wheeled cultivators were pushed by might and main through the rows. At least two Aftonites, Harold Van Alstine and the late Roy Johnson, recalled their youthful struggles with this slow and tedious work at the Berglund farm.

RUBY AND REG MILLS, INEZ AND CHAUNCEY VAN ALSTINE, AT THE VAN ALSTINE FARM ABOUT 1950.

After harvesting, the onions were dried on the third and fourth floors of the "onion house," the fifty-six-foot long building that Dave and Sandy today use as their garage. The onion house, vintage 1914-1915, served multiple purposes: machinery was weather-protected on the first floor; the next level served as a granary; the top two levels consisted of spaced laths on which the onions were spread out in such a way as to allow maximum air circulation between the laths.

Though outnumbered by the men, the Berglund women worked just as hard at making the farm profitable, planting enough strawberry plants to supply customers in several midwestern states. Poultry and egg preparation were also added to the usual indoor work of the women. Elvera Berglund brightened evenings at home by playing the organ and the piano. Finally the family acquired the ultimate instrument—a player piano. Elvera also occasionally played the piano for programs at the Swedish Methodist Church in the village.

Somewhat surprisingly, of the eight Berglund children, only two of them—Arthur and Emmett—left the family circle to start their own families. Both of these young men were drafted during World War I; after returning home to Afton and marrying, they settled their families no more than two miles from their parental homestead. "The rest of the family was clearly upset by what they considered their desertion," said Sandy Berglund. But Arthur and Emmett were always available to lend a helping hand, and the four brothers from the farm returned their help when called.

Emmett married Flora Lambrecht in 1928. He farmed briefly, but then turned more enthusiastically to carpentry. His apprenticeship had been served at the home farm where he and brother Edwin had remodeled the house and built all of the other structures, such as the onion house, two chicken houses, storage sheds, and the dairy barn. Emmett and Flora's son Donald and his wife Laura today live on St. Paul's east side.

After saving his money, Arthur Berglund married Faith Canfield in 1929 and bought his own farm in the spring of that year two miles south of the Oak Grove farm on the Afton-Denmark town line. Arthur and Faith had four children—Harold, David (who now owns his grandparents' homestead), Martha, and Audrey. All of Dave's siblings live with their families within a close radius of the Oak Grove farm.

When Charles Berglund died in 1941, the eldest son, Fred, took the helm of the farm. A voracious reader on many subjects, he also loved music and taught himself to play the violin. "Fred Berglund was a real genius," remarked Harold Van Alstine, "but he never was able to obtain patents for his inventions." Some of these inventions, for instance, were an applicator for shaving cream cans and an adjustable pencil sharpener.

By 1970 only the aging Fred and Herbert, by then eighty-two and sixty-six respectively, were left to carry on, and most of the farm's 265 acres were rented out. "In fact," said nephew Dave Berglund, "by the time Grandfather Charles died, the farm had already begun to lose much of its drive and direction." Fred and Herbert, though sixteen years apart in age, died within six months of each other—Herbert in November 1984 and Fred in June 1985.

Like a living organism, the Berglund's Oak Grove farm had completed its first cycle and passed into history. Looking back on the family's accomplishments, Dave and Sandy Berglund suggest that it was the family's high principles, their unbending morality, and their fierce work ethic that were responsible for their survival and success in those difficult days.

Today, as with most old farms in the area, much of the Oak Grove acreage has been sold for development. Extremely attractive building sites surrounded by hills and woods and close to the great river have been improved by Mark Olmstead and his Valliswood Associates. That part of the farm retained by Dave and Sandy, rescued from the ravages of time, celebrates the spirit and body of the pioneer farm. Grandparents Charles and Martha and the uncles and aunts who poured their lives into Oak Grove must be very pleased.

AFTON ROAD CREW IN VALLEY CREEK AREA, EARLY 1900S.

MARY
PENNINGTON

Gordy and Kathy Jarvis bought the Afton House in 1976, but it had long been the old village hotel, starting as the Cushing Hotel in 1867. This Cushing structure is said to have been built around a house belonging to one of three Thomas brothers who were among the first settlers in Afton.

The very first Afton hotel, however, had been the Paterson House on the west side of Washington Street in 1856. Stagecoaches brought guests to this stylish establishment, and workers in the sawmill at Glenmont often crossed the St. Croix River to board there. When this structure burned in 1861, hotelkeeper S.J. Paterson opened Afton's first store on the same site—the present location of the old Richert house, which is now painted yellow and most recently was an antique store.

The Cushing hotel, built by Civil War veteran Charles C. Cushing, meanwhile, has endured more than 125 years, although altered with varying degrees of success by several different restauranteurs since World War II. Long before the renovations, however, when the hotel loomed barn-like and often unpainted, one owner, Mary Lange Pennington, stood out for her long tenure (1907-1945) and unrivaled record of dogged physical labor.

What did the old Afton Hotel look like in the Pennington era? Imagine the present building minus the large dining room. Also take away the Catfish Saloon and the new second story addition. Tack onto the rear at the northeast side an open, square porch and add a longer screened porch across the Washington Street front. Above the front porch hang a plain sign lettered simply, "HOTEL," and you have Mary Pennington's establishment.

As "summer people" living at Catfish Bar, my family sometimes drove from Minneapolis to the Afton Hotel for meals before crossing the river. Mary Pennington's sumptuous chicken dinners became a happy habit for many people like us from the Twin Cities and elsewhere. And even after sixty years, the sights, sounds, and smells of

CLEAN-UP DAY AT THE METHODIST CHURCH. LEFT TO RIGHT: REV. BEDFORD, MARY PENNINGTON, MRS. SANDERSON, MRS. SWANLUND, MRS. BENSON, UNIDENTIFIED, MARY CHRISTIANSON. THIS PICTURE WAS TAKEN IN FRONT OF MARY PENNINGTON'S HOTEL AFTER THE WOMEN HAD FINISHED THEIR WORK.

Mrs. Pennington's hotel still live in my memory.

We entered through the front porch to the large parlor (at least it seemed large then) cluttered with unmatched furniture and showing a kind of faded elegance. An upright piano stood against the northwest wall. Substituting for indoor plumbing, a washstand with sink, pitcher of water, bowl, soap, and drain emptying into a pail underneath lined the opposite wall.

The dining room to the east was a spacious, bright area with three or four long tables running north and south, covered with white linen. Atop them stood jelly glasses filled with cowslips, the local name for marigolds, and other flowers from Mary's big garden. That cheery room was permeated by an ambrosia of smells—Mary's woodburning stove, her fresh-baked bread, and all of the other fragrances of her cooking.

From where we sat eating by the windows, we could see chickens fussing over their feed in the yard. In the middle of the yard was the well with its long-handled pump. Mrs. Pennington would pump the handle up and down and lug heavy pails of water into the kitchen. I did not know then how chickens were killed, so when I happened to see Mary snatch one up and chop off its head on a tree stump, it left a disturbing memory.

Attached to the north wall of the dining room was the old-time telephone with its little shelf for taking notes. As we ate our dinner, this phone rang frequently with its sporadic longs and shorts. We urban children did not understand the rural phone system with its party lines and listeners. We were puzzled that usually no one bothered to answer it; we did not know that one picked up the receiver only after hearing his own signal.

74

Many years later, I became acquainted with the remarkable Arthur Brown who, with his family, was the whole Washington County Rural Telephone Company. Art served as both "central" and repairman, scaling the poles in ice storms to reattach broken wires. As central, he was the friendly fount of all knowledge. If you failed to reach a neighbor, he might say, "Oh, Linda's over at Kate's having coffee."

The girls who worked for Mary Pennington, including her great-niece Marion Schmegal, granddaughter Loraine Billy, and stepdaughter Florence Johnson, summoned guests from the parlor when dinner was ready and placed on the tables large platters of chicken, bowls of mashed potatoes with gravy, vegetables, corn on the cob, strawberry preserves, and relish. No meal ever lacked homemade white and brown bread. Dessert was usually Mary's homemade ice cream, apple or lemon meringue pie, or blitz tort. Retired Afton barber Harold Sill said, "I used to turn the crank of her ice cream freezer on the back porch."

Mary Pennington stood barely five feet tall and wore her thinning white hair in a pug high on the back of her head. Her demeanor was always cheerful, and once the meal was under way, she would leave her battle station in the kitchen to visit for a few minutes with guests. Speaking with just the trace of an accent, she pronounced St. Paul, "Sin Paul," intending no pun. Tennis shoes eased a bit the ache in her feet, which seldom knew rest.

This tiny woman married three times and had two daughters, Hazel Pennington Billy and Mabel North Baskin. Granddaughter Loraine Billy Allen, who now lives in California, spent a lot of time with Mary

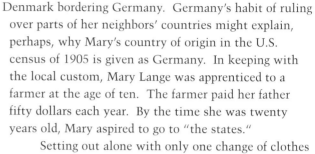

*MY PARENTS WALTER
AND ESTHER ROBB,
JULY 1952.*

and knew her well. "Grandma didn't talk much about the past, almost as if some of it were too painful," said Mrs. Allen. When I talked with Marion Schmegal, she told me, "Well, whatever you write, write it with love."

Loraine Billy Allen believes her grandmother was born Mary Lange in that part of Denmark bordering Germany. Germany's habit of ruling over parts of her neighbors' countries might explain, perhaps, why Mary's country of origin in the U.S. census of 1905 is given as Germany. In keeping with the local custom, Mary Lange was apprenticed to a farmer at the age of ten. The farmer paid her father fifty dollars each year. By the time she was twenty years old, Mary aspired to go to "the states."

Setting out alone with only one change of clothes and a basket of food, Mary expected a relative to meet her in America. On arrival, she found no one, and she was forced to take refuge in an institution for homeless girls. Next she worked for an American gentlemen whose son, Mrs. Allen says, took a shine to Mary and often asked her to accompany him on rides in the buggy. What became of this suitor we don't know.

Long years after that, perhaps after living for a time in Maine, Mary eventually ended up in northwestern Minnesota where she was the first postmaster in that area with a little hole-in-the-wall kind of post office. Mrs. Allen thinks there is some connection between the name of Pennington County and Mary's second husband, Charles Pennington.

Mary's first husband was named Newarck, now pronounced North. Their daughter, Mabel North, married Bert Baskin, a prominent Afton resident who was the local railroad depot agent and a member of the Afton Citizens' State Bank board of directors. I can remember seeing Bert occasionally sitting on the steps of the present Lerk's Bar when he sometimes filled in as proprietor for Swan Hallberg about 1937. He invariably wore a long-sleeved shirt, even in the summer, with a stiff, starched collar but no tie. Bert and Mabel North Baskin had two daughters, Loraine and Edith.

Mary Pennington was also married to a man named McGrath, but this was evidently a brief marriage. Mary's stepdaughter, Florence Johnson, was the daughter of McGrath and a former wife. After Mary's separation from McGrath, she reclaimed the name Pennington.

Mary's daughter Hazel Pennington married Wilford Joseph Billy. Their children were Loraine, Roger, Ray, John, Patricia, Wallace, Andre, Larry, and Trudy. During the years we went to the hotel, I remember seeing Hazel, Loraine, and the first three boys—Roger, Ray, and John. While Loraine helped her grandmother, the boys, who were then less than ten, obediently kept to themselves to avoid getting in the way of guests.

MAE CLYMER AND LINDA HALLQUIST IN FRONT OF THE OLD GARAGE (WHICH NOW HOUSES THE POST OFFICE) IN THE 1920S.

Upstairs in her hotel, Mrs. Pennington rented rooms to several boarders including Matt Rafferty, who ran the grain elevator and, like Baskin, was a bank director. Another was a man named Riley. The door to the second floor stairway was in the dining room, and at mealtime, Mrs. Pennington would step to the door and yell up the stairway, "RILEY!" Thus summoned, Riley would descend and take his place at the long table with us. A balding man with a large, bushy mustache, which town gossips said he blackened with shoe polish, he worked at clearing land and grubbing stumps. Possessed of an encyclopedic knowledge

HAROLD "LERK" LIND IN
THE 1930S ON THE STEPS
OF THE CONFECTIONERY
STORE THAT HE TURNED
INTO A BAR AND GRILL
AFTER PROHIBITION
WAS REPEALED.

of baseball history, he liked to hold forth on the subject in his deep, resonant voice.

Betty Lu Anderson Crocombe, who grew up in the house across Washington Street where Mary Ann Scroggins now lives, remembers often staying overnight at the hotel with Mary's granddaughter Loraine. "Carrying flickering kerosene lamps up that narrow flight of steps as they cast their shadows across the walls was always romantic, and we'd study our lessons together." For her part, Loraine recalls her own excitement when invited to stay at the Anderson home. "The best thing," she said, "was that they had a radio so we could listen to our favorite programs."

One summer evening, when my parents and one of my brothers and I returned to Afton to cross the river to our place, a strong south wind was whipping the St. Croix River into frenzied whitecaps. Deciding our crossing might be chancy, my father arranged for us to stay the night in the hotel. We were comfortable enough, I remember, but alarmed at the method for a speedy egress in case of fire; at the side of the window hung a large loop of heavy rope. Evidently, if fire broke out, we were to grab that rope and swing out of the window down to the street below.

Loraine Allen tells a story revealing the confined life Mary Pennington lived in her hotel. During the middle 1930s when football coach Bernie Bierman led his University of Minnesota teams to several consecutive national championships, Bierman regularly sequestered his teams on pre-game Friday nights at the popular White Pine Inn in nearby Bayport. My father was an avid Bierman and Minnesota football fan and wanted Mary to meet a few of these national champions. Somehow he arranged for them to be driven from Bayport to Afton one Friday. Loraine did not describe the entire scene but said, "When it was all over and they had gone, Grandma took me aside and asked, 'What's football?'"

Mrs. Pennington's life was not completely monastic, however, and she did enjoy a limited social life. She loved her friends, who were all devoted to her, and served with great faithfulness the little Afton Methodist-Episcopal Church, where she belonged to the Ladies' Aid. For recreation in her rare, quieter times, she liked to play Chinese checkers with her friends. One of her regular guests for visits and coffee was Myrta Morey Siebolds, a widow who years later became the mother-in-law of famed World War II correspondent Ernie Pyle.

An Afton notable who helped make her village a welcoming haven to natives and tourists alike, Mary Pennington died in 1945. There is a large Pennington monument in Evergreen Cemetery with individuals stones for Mary and Charles, their daughter Hazel Pennington Billy, and a grandson, Ray Billy. At the Afton House, the Jarvises have remembered their spunky predecessor by naming their smaller dining room, "The Pennington Room."

SWEDE HILL NEIGHBORS

n 1945, looking back on his long and venturesome life, Afton pioneer Tom Cooney published a small autobiography titled *Meet Tom Cooney*. Tom dedicated his book to his "Sincere Friend and Good Neighbor, Oliver E. Charley," who contributed the Preface. "Few men living today," Charley wrote, "have experienced as much of the colorful and varied life of the pioneer as our friend and neighbor—TOM COONEY. . . .

> *Child immigrant from England, early settler-of-the-soil, scholar, civil engineer for the newly-organized Northern Pacific and Great Northern Railways, Timber Cruiser, Miner, Prospector, Authority on soils and minerals, Officer in the United States Army—these are some of the highlights in the work of this grand old man. . . .*

> *And today, in his spacious farm home, just south of Afton, Minnesota, one may find Tom, at ninety-two, still alert and active in mind and body, seated by a cheerful fire in the fireplace and, between puffs on his favorite pipe, reminiscing in his kindly, humorous fashion over his colorful past now rich in pleasant memories.*

Tom Cooney was born December 18, 1853, in Chester, England, to James and Mary Dunn Cooney. Two older sisters, Annie and Ellen, watched their little brother Tom at play on the Roman walls built two thousands years earlier. Immersed thus in history, Tom in his active imagination romanticized the past, visioning "the great runners and the fine chariots and horses of that era." Ahead of him stretched an equally romantic future.

Tom's father James Cooney was an Irishman who fulfilled his own dream of the future by emigrating to New York in 1854. Making his way west, he worked one season in a Wisconsin lumber camp before setting off on foot for Galena, Illinois, where he hoped to find work in the lead mines. By some stroke of good fortune, he stopped at the Bolles' gristmill in Afton for a drink of water. There he met Warren Getchell, who convinced him to spend the winter in Afton, working on his place. In the spring, Getchell told James, he would help him get started farming.

After five years' separation from James, Mary Cooney with Tom and his sisters arrived in Afton in May 1859. The little frame house that stood waiting for them near the Getchell farm on Swede Hill had one large room downstairs that served as living room, dining room, and kitchen; a small room off it was Tom's parents' bedroom. Tom and his sisters slept in an unfinished room upstairs. "It was wonderful how homelike my mother made our home with our meagre belongings," Tom remembered. During the three years the Cooneys lived there, Tom's sister Lizzie was born in 1860. Subsequently, James Cooney bought the "40" that the family always afterward called home from a lawyer named Heatherington for two hundred dollars.

Tom worked all his growing-up years on the family farm (which was located approximately where Esco Obermann used to live at 14754 50th Street). For a time, Tom and his sisters attended the Haskell School, taught by a lame woman named Miss Bangs. During the Civil War, when Tom's father served two years with the Union Army, the children stayed home winters. "Frankly, we didn't have enough warm clothes," Tom recalled. "But we managed to keep fairly comfortable at home, and spring brought us an abundance of sunshine and wild fruits, wild strawberries, red and black raspberries, and gooseberries; and later on there were wild plums and crabs. Whole areas grew up in blueberries."

Later on, Tom Cooney attended the yellow brick St. Croix Valley Academy in Afton, where he learned the basics of surveying, but after the first semester, he was needed at home on the farm. "There was never more than a hundred names on the roster of the Academy, but I shall always feel a warmth of remembrance for it," he wrote. In 1874, when he was twenty-one, Tom entered the University of Minnesota to study engineering. There was then only one building on the campus— "Old Blue Stone." When Tom returned home to Afton, generally on weekends, he walked the entire thirty miles. "The city walking was

THIS OCTAGON BARN AT THE CORNER OF NEAL AVENUE AND AFTON BOULEVARD (HWY. 95) WAS AN AFTON LANDMARK UNTIL IT BURNED IN APRIL 1988.

actually pleasant; but many of the country roads had not been broken by teams, and the going was heavy."

One of Tom's most endearing traits was his sensitivity to the beauties and wonder of nature, and like Oliver Charley, he especially loved birds.

I watched the grouse all one season [he wrote in *Meet Tom Cooney*], *from early spring when they feasted on the hazel corks (some folks called them tassels), and sought succulent basswood, willow, and birch buds, to late fall, when the storms were upon them.*

The grouse lived under the snow in the winter—he had watched Indians tracking them to their hiding places—but quail were less canny, and he felt sorry for this "southern gentleman [which] does not have [an] inbred knowledge of how to fight extreme cold."

JOSEPH AND MARY OLDHAM WITH SON HARRY IN FRONT OF THEIR HOME ON TRADING POST TRAIL, 1920S. JOE OLDHAM WAS A BOYHOOD FRIEND AND NEIGHBOR OF TOM COONEY'S IN AFTON. IN THE LATE 1870S, BOTH MEN HAD TAKEN UP CLAIMS IN THE RED RIVER VALLEY.

He will put his beak under the breast of the one in front of him, standing close to his neighbor, hopeful that the warmth of a whole covey will be enough to keep adequate heat in each feathery body. Several times I have found a little covey of quail standing in this formation, frozen stiff. I have shed many a tear over these gentlefolk.

Going off from Afton, Tom lived a life of adventure as a landowner and schoolteacher in Dakota Territory (where his pupils ranged in age from six to sixteen and were "mostly Norwegians"); as a civil engineer and surveyor in buffalo country; as a timber cruiser in the northern forests; as a first lieutenant of an engineering battalion during the Spanish-American War; and finally, as a land agent for the Northern Pacific Railroad.

In his retirement, Tom Cooney, who had never married, returned to Afton—his "green valley," he called it—where he put out the welcome mat for his many friends. "These cool evenings you'll find a crackling log fire lighting up the hunting trophies on his big living room walls," wrote St. Paul paper columnist Paul Light. His six-hundred-acre farm included the tract his father had purchased in the 1850s.

Tom's good friend on Swede Hill, Oliver Charley, was a generation younger than Tom, but both men shared a deep love of their river valley and all its wildlife. Both men, too, viewed their existence on the planet with a philosophical mixture of pleasure and pain—pleasure in nature's bounty, and pain in watching it being destroyed by man.

Oliver Charley was born on the family farm in Kellogg, Minnesota, May 30, 1892. In 1919 he drove his horse and buggy from Lake City, Minnesota, to his new home in Afton. The magnets attracting Charley to this valley were the steep, green bluffs of

OLIVER AND FRIEDA CHARLEY LIVED ON BLUFF-TOP ACREAGE LATER DEVELOPED INTO AFTON STATE PARK. A LOVER OF AFTON'S BEAUTY, HE WAS A GOOD STEWARD OF THE LAND.

85

summer and the broad, blue river. His ninety-six acres cost ten dollars an acre, and as farmland, it was not the most productive. As scenic property, however, it later sold for up to ten thousand dollars an acre— the hottest real estate in this part of the country. At the time of Oliver's purchase, neighboring farmers scoffed, "You can't live off the scenery."

Raising a few head of cattle, some hay, and soybeans, Oliver concentrated more on his link with nature than on an attempt to pump the soil for profit. A big, complex farm that brought wealth would have kept him from roaming his fields and hills—observing, probing, filming, and just relishing the riches he found around him. Like Henry David Thoreau, he was far happier examining the habits of wild creatures and discovering rare species of plants than tending crops. And like Thoreau, he built a small but slightly more elaborate cabin in addition to his house; perched high on the hill above the St. Croix, it mirrored Oliver's wish to escape the world's clamor.

As a conservationist, Oliver Charley practiced strip farming and crop rotation when these were new techniques. In 1923 he hired a crew to plant ten thousand tree seedlings to halt soil erosion. Two decades later, he participated in a large tree-planting program under the Soil Conservation District.

Among his many services to the environment, however, Oliver's work with bluebirds commanded the highest respect. Beginning in 1925 Oliver started building bluebird houses and setting them out in what is now Afton State Park. He probably originated the first bluebird trail in the state—possibly in the country. (The bluebird houses on a bluebird trail are monitored by checking on birds, cleaning their houses, and recording their populations.) Commenting on these little friends he loved so much, Oliver said, "Their spring song is sweet and happy while their fall song is sad and melancholy. They just don't like to leave this beautiful valley."

Afton historian David Haslund called Oliver "a modern Will Rogers, farmer, philosopher, realist, and dreamer." Once while Oliver and Dave were standing on the hill admiring Oliver's unbroken view of the river, Oliver remarked, "From here you can see everything but prosperity, and that's just around the corner."

Thanks to Robert "Boz" Metsdorf, a former musician turned naturalist and film-maker, and Boz's partner, Mike Leitner, we have glimpses of Oliver's life on video tape. Boz had viewed some of Oliver's nature films and become enthralled with the man—his quiet dignity, his ready wit, and his old-fashioned morality. In "The Oliver Charley Story," which can be seen at the Afton Historical Museum, he skillfully blended biography with Oliver's own pictures of flowers, birds, and animals.

In the last scene of the video tape, Oliver, then nine-four years old, smiles, waves goodbye, and walks for the last time through the stone gate to his farm. The Charley farm had been acquired for Afton State Park, and Oliver and his wife Frieda were leaving his beloved Bluebird Hill for the last time. A few days after this filming, the fire department torched the farmhouse, barn, and other outbuildings.

Carrying on work he learned from Oliver, Boz Metsdorf later worked as a volunteer manager of the bluebird trail at Afton State Park. When he took on the project in 1992, he tended fifty nest boxes on the northern end of the park and to the west on Oliver's former land. Boz thinks Afton State Park has the highest concentration of bluebirds in the nation!

An Afton resident for sixty-two years, Oliver Charley died May 7, 1993, a few weeks shy of his 101st birthday. Somewhat curiously, there was an unexplained drop in the bluebird population that season. Early spring ice storms may have destroyed some of the birds before they finished their migration here, but it seems sadly appropriate that so many of Oliver's little blue friends failed to return that year to their summer home in Afton. It was almost as if they knew he was no longer there.

AN 1895
WALKING TOUR

L et's imagine a time warp in which we step back into Afton a century ago to walk its streets and examine the village. To keep our tour within reasonable limits, let's stay mostly inside the old village—that part of Afton tourists know best. To further simplify things, we'll refer to the current street names and addresses, although these are different from the ones on the original plat.

Commencing our walk at the north end of the village where St. Croix Trail bends northeast and Stagecoach Trail takes its more westerly route north, we first see the St. Paulus German Lutheran Cemetery with its earliest burial in 1886. Oddly, neither the German church nor its parsonage are there yet. The church will be moved in from another site about 1910 and then razed in 1947; the parsonage at 3032 So. St. Croix Trail, immediately in front of the cemetery, will be built in 1910.

Continuing south to 31st Street, turn right and walk west to Perrot Avenue, where we come to a smallish, story-and-a-half house occupied in 1895 by one of the many Spreeman families, this one with eighteen children. Later it will become the home of the George Briggs, Jr. family.

Moving out to St. Croix Trail again, we come to Afton's principal landmark—the Afton Public School which had first been the 1868 St. Croix Valley Academy and then in 1884, Luther Seminary, a German Lutheran institution of the Joint Synod of Ohio.

Then turn west onto Afton Boulevard from St. Croix Trail. On the right side of the street, we come to the Pete Peterson or "Onion Pete" house at 15894 Afton Blvd. A Swedish immigrant who moved to Afton in 1882, Pete worked first for the Milwaukee Railroad and then raised fruits and vegetables west of the village. His success with onions accounts for the nickname. During World War I, Dr. George Herman Burfiend, Afton's doctor, will live and practice medicine in this house until moving to St. Paul in 1920.

Next door stands the 1893 Swedish Methodist-Episcopal Church parsonage (which in the 1980s will be moved to a new site on So. St. Croix Trail), and beside it, the steepled church itself. Founded by Methodists from the old "Mounds Prairie" or "Townline Church" on Afton Township's western boundary, this church was constructed in 1886.

Continuing west up Afton Boulevard and turning left onto Pennington Avenue, we see on the right, perched atop the high knoll, a frame house. The original owner's name has eluded us, but in the 1950s Myron and Kirk Franz will live in this home with its watchtower-like view of the St. Croix.

A bit south on Pennington, set far back from the street on the right, we view the spacious Nels Rosenquist house where that large family was nurtured. Lying a short distance outside the village boundary on the west, it was here as early as the 1870s.

After the Rosenquist house, Pennington has no more homes on either side until we come to the 1880s house in which Charles and Millie Nelson lived many years. (This house will be razed following Millie's death in 1959.) Then, with one more place, the George Briggs, Sr. berry farm at 3404 Pennington Avenue, which also falls on the township side of the boundary, we have completed our tour of Pennington Avenue.

Let's turn around now and follow Pennington back to Afton Boulevard, turn right, go down the hill, and take another right onto Perrot Avenue. On the west side at 3160 Perrot is the Peter Paulson house, dating to 1891. Peter and his wife Marie had eight children. Next door to the south is the Swanson-Kallstrom house, another 1880s place. Its 1895 owner is not known, but in the late 1920s and 1930s it will be occupied by Harry and Marion Swanson, who though blind, will keep their independence in various amazing ways. Besides making twine door mats, Harry will cane furniture and help distribute candy for the Goggins Candy Company. Following World War II, Harlan and Viliss Granberg Kallstrom will raise three children in this house.

Head north again on Perrot to Afton Boulevard and turn right to St. Croix Trail. Near the corner of St. Croix Trail and Afton Blvd., we see storekeeper Paul Frederick's home, constructed by Richard Buswell in 1859; this house will later be moved to Perrot and 32nd Street. Frederick's store, built about the same time, stands just south of his home. The only traces of this store that will remain in the 1990s are remnants of its concrete foundation.

Then, on the corner of 32nd Street and St. Croix Trail, we come to the dwelling of Congregationalist minister Rev. Simon Putnam, Afton's first resident preacher and school superintendent, who taught school in the kitchen of his parsonage. This parsonage will later be reincarnated as "the little red house."

Across 32nd Street from the parsonage is the house erected by Afton patriarch William Thomas in 1857 and once lived in by pioneer S.H. Paterson who established Afton's first hotel a block away on the corner of 33rd Street and St. Croix Trail. In the 1850s Thomas's blacksmith shop stood behind his house. Farther down the block is Afton's oldest house, built by Andrew Mackey in 1841 (which in the 1990s will house Baglio's clothing shop and the Afton Toy Shop).

THE AFTON BAND ABOUT 1920 ON THE STEPS OF THE CITIZENS' STATE BANK. DR. GEORGE BURFIEND IS SECOND FROM LEFT.

Turning west on 33rd Street at the Mackey house and approaching the point where the hill starts its climb, we come to the tiny Swan Hallberg home where the bachelor lives with his sister Emma and later, her two sons, Clifford and Leonard Luzar.

Back on St. Croix Trail again and continuing south, we find the two-story house of German immigrant Ferdinand Richert, dating to 1890. This site was formerly occupied by Afton's first hotel, the stylish but short-lived Paterson House, at whose door visitors alighted from stagecoaches. Built in 1856, the Paterson House burned down in 1861. Directly south of the Richert house is Ferdinand's store which in 1895 houses the Foss-Armstrong Hardware Store. Next door to the south is the home of pioneer Benjamin Pelham Squires, who erected this house in 1874 and carried mail. Squires had earlier operated a store in South Afton.

Slightly west of the Squires house, facing the park, stands one of Afton's early schools. A small brick building with a bell tower, it was constructed in 1876 at a cost of five hundred dollars. Across the street, the one-block-square Afton Park, platted as part of the village in 1855, has not yet been embellished by any structures.

South of the park, on the corner of St. Croix Trail and Upper 34th Street, is the house, rather grand for its day, constructed by founding settler Charles S. Getchell, then occupied through the years by others who served as Afton postmasters while operating the store next door. Earlier, the William Tilton house stood on this site; Tilton lived here from 1857 to 1860 when he operated a sawmill with a partner named Newman in the area that will much later become Steamboat Park. On the corner of St. Croix Trail and 35th Street is the 1859 house built by Civil War veteran Joseph Dernley, who owned a greenhouse on his property and rented out rooms in his house.

Walking west on 35th Street, we see on the north side the house of Andrew Sjoholm, a wagon maker who works with blacksmith Chris Christensen. The house across from the Sjoholm place on the south belongs to John and Nellie Peterson. After John dies, Nellie will marry August Olson in 1914. This property will belong to descendants of John and Nellie Peterson until the middle 1980s. East of these two houses at 15895 35th Street is the roomy, two-story house lived in by the Fred and Ida Johnson family who are there, we believe, in 1895; later Frank and Irene Spreeman and their children will occupy this house into the 1980s.

Slightly north and east of the Johnson-Spreeman house stands the saloon put up by Stillwater brewer Joseph Wolf in the late 1880s. Saloon keepers included a Mr. Meyer, Paul Gedatus, "Long John" Nyquist, and Swan Hallberg. Long John Nyquist reportedly propped a loaded shotgun against the bar, accidentally bumped it, and caused his own death. For a time in the 1920s George Slater will own the saloon and employ Joe Hayner as barkeep.

Going west on 36th Street, toward Gummeson's Coulee (named for Civil War veteran Clement Gummeson who lived there with his wife Clara in the 1880s), we come to the site, at least, of Afton Village's first school alongside the little Gummeson's Creek flowing out of the coulee.

FRED AND IDA ROSENQUIST JOHNSON LIVED THEIR ENTIRE LIVES IN AFTON. FRED WORKED FOR THE RAILROAD, AND IDA TENDED MANY AILING RESIDENTS.

Then, entering the deep, shaded coulee, we come to two houses, both of which show signs of long occupancy but whose history is unknown. Leaving the coulee and traveling east, we see on the right side the Thorvald Holberg house, owned by the parents of Clarence, Herbert, and Ed Holberg, Selma Swanson's husband.

On the corner of 36th Street and St. Croix Trail stands the simple but sturdy little house built by Ernest Nelson in 1882. When Nelson died in 1892, his widow married John Hedstrom. The Hedstroms will live here until 1919, then move across the street. Later Milbert and Lillie Nelson Clymer and Ray and Luella Clymer will live here and raise their families until 1976. The Clymers are descended from George L. Clymer, the well-to-do

Pennsylvania farmer who helped finance the American Revolutionary War and signed the Declaration of Independence.

A block farther south, at 37th Street and St. Croix Trail, we find the house of Asa Tracy, a shingle-maker, who built it soon after arriving in Afton in 1857. Finally, walking past 37th Street, we see a house set back from the road to the west atop a rise covered with blue spruce trees. Frank and Alma Osterlind from the Twin Cities will later live in this house, followed by the L'Alliers; Roland L'Allier was an F.B.I. agent.

At the south end of Afton where St. Croix Trail curves to the right and the River Road forks left, we meet a large white house with soft green trim and shutters known as the Charles V. Johnson home. Pioneer settler Andrew Mackey once owned it, and Mary Pennington later lived there and ran it as a boarding house before selling it to Johnson. Both Charles and his brother "Willie" Johnson were native, longtime inhabitants of Afton.

Turning around and starting up St. Croix Trail toward the north, we note that the first house on the right at 3601 So. St. Croix Trail belongs at this early period to Andrew Nord who has his blacksmith shop south of the house. Nord has attached a rip and sawmill to his shop, south of which he also has a feed mill. The house will later be occupied by Albert and Lydia Brown Swanson.

Next north we see a small house beside the creek lived in by Magnus Hedstrom, who was actuary and treasurer of the Evergreen Cemetery Board for twenty-four years. In 1859 a Negro woman named Jenny Peters from New York lived there and did laundry piece work for the villagers.

Just north of the creek at 3561 So. St. Croix Trail, the Ole Thueson place is even smaller. Schoolteacher Alma Augusta Johnson lived here from 1882 to 1893; in 1895 Thueson operates it casually as a boarding house for single working men who enjoy their liquor together after a strenuous day of building cisterns, clearing land, or grubbing stumps.

Our following stop brings us to the 1850s house originally belonging to Charlie Root, whose past is a mystery. Afton barber Herbert Sill and his wife Clara will live here later before moving to Lake St. Croix Beach in 1945. Sill will stucco this house, the only place in Afton then to have such protection. After World War II Robert Greer, a retired railroad employee, and his wife Mabel will reside here. Eventually the house will be dismantled by woodcarver Elmo "the Builder" Erickson and replaced by the old Swedish Methodist-Episcopal parsonage.

Turn right on 35th Street, cross over the railroad tracks, and we come to the small house Swen Parson's family has lived in since 1880, the year they came from Sweden. Directly across 35th Street stands the Fred Korth frame house. Korth will work for the L.L. May Nursery a few years hence. Years later, his house will be replaced by a two-story home built by Leonard Nordstrom, who was raised with his several brothers in Afton.

Back on St. Croix Trail, the next house at 3491 So. St. Croix Trail is one of Afton's oldest and most substantial structures. Through the years, its many occupants important to Afton history will include storekeeper Joe Hayner and his family, and Afton mayors Roy Johnson and Henry Sommer; Sommer will also manage the Inter-State Lumber Company yard.

Before coming to the next house, we see a clearing at the riverside where the Tilton and Newman sawmill existed for only three years beginning in 1857. This clearing also marked a common landing for steamboats in those years.

Continuing north on St. Croix Trail, we note that Selma's Ice Cream Parlor-to-be is just a residence in 1895; constructed in 1880, it belongs to the Holbergs, Selma's in-laws. Just north of Selma's is what will later be called the George Benson house when the Bensons move off their farm south of Afton and into the village. In 1895, however, Charles Pennington owns this property. Next door is Chris Christensen's 1890s blacksmith shop, which he will operate into the 1930s.

Having now arrived at what residents consider the "center of town," we learn that our first house on the east side belongs to William and Mathilda Olson Picullel. Mrs. Picullel will occupy this old, unpainted dwelling into the 1930s. Back of the Picullel house to the east are two Indian mounds which pre-date the Dakota or Sioux Indians by several hundred years.

THE AFTON HOTEL BUILT BY CIVIL WAR VETERAN CHARLES C. CUSHING IN 1867. OVER TIME THIS STRUCTURE WILL EVOLVE INTO THE AFTON HOUSE INN.

The Afton Garage-cum-post office, the barber shop, Lerk's, the brick bank building—none of these have yet made their appearance in 1895. Our next stop, then, at the corner of St. Croix Trail and 33rd Street, is the Cushing Hotel, Afton's second hotel, which envelops a house Miner Thomas erected in 1859. North of the Cushing Hotel, on the next corner, is Afton's first store. Built first as a house, its small commercial wing was added onto it by Meredith Thomas. Meredith was the son of pioneer settler William Thomas and grew up with his siblings Miner and Hewit in the present Scroggins house.

Turning right on 32nd Street, we approach the river landing where Frank Spreeman, Sr. runs his fishing and boat rental business. An about-face and walk to the west again over the railroad tracks brings us to the large, white house erected by town father Charles S. Getchell in 1859. Then, returning to St. Croix Trail, we are struck at once by the unusual shape of the large, octagonal house on the corner. Constructed in 1856 by the energetic Meredith Thomas, it was used for a time after 1868 as an overflow dormitory for the St. Croix Valley Academy. It also served as a home for Rev. Henry Ernst who became president of Luther Seminary beginning in 1885. In 1895 Frank and Minnie Spreeman live here and will for many years to come.

Just north of his octagon house, Frank Spreeman, who was Afton's lamplighter of long ago, has put up a little shop where Mrs. Spreeman sells smoked carp and buffalo fish, and fresh pike, pickerel, and catfish. The painted outline of a fish on the screened porch advertises its St. Croix produce. Next to the Spreeman fish shop and dwarfing it is the high-ceilinged Congregational church, built in 1868 but rented by the American Methodists in 1895.

MRS. FRANK (MUTTA OR MINNIE) SPREEMAN ON THE SWING IN THE YARD OF HER OCTAGON HOUSE.

Across from the church building at 15904 Afton Blvd. is the home of Rev. W.D. Ahl, a faculty member with long and distinguished teaching service at Luther Seminary. In 1895, however, it seems certain the residents are Chris and Amelia Lind. Their many children included Martin Chris Lind who would raise his own large family just up the street.

Turning east on Afton Blvd. toward the river, we see the Richard Spreeman-Henry Kane house down near the old river pasture. Richard was a cousin of Bert, Frank, and Emil Spreeman; Marion Kane, a sister of Hazel Mullen Briggs, moved here to the village from the southern part of the township. An Ole Swenson is reported to have built this house in 1882.

If we next walk north on Pike Street, which is scarcely a street at all, and turn left on 31st Street

to go west, we come to the town's first lumber yard, fronting St. Croix Trail. This yard was in operation by 1895 but will burn sometime before 1900.

Across 31st Street from the lumber yard on the north stands the house where Martin and Emma Lind, who came to Afton from Sweden, he in 1882, she in 1886, will begin their married life in 1896. Who is living here in 1895 we don't know. The Lind children will include Harold "Lerk" Lind who will put Afton on the map with his "Lerkburger."

Now, for the last leg of our walk, let's do an about-face and head east along 31st Street toward the river. The Stillwater-Hastings Railroad laid its tracks here in 1882, and Afton has its own depot along with a windmill-topped water tank for servicing the locomotives. Near the tracks also is the Jamieson Company elevator, constructed before 1900.

This, then, is how Afton appeared five years before the end of the last century.

THE JAMIESON ELEVATOR UNDER CONSTRUCTION. IT LATER BELONGED TO THE J.D. DILL COMPANY.

ONE CENTURY
LATER

Retracing our steps, we find that old Afton has changed—but slowly and undramatically. Although the new city of Afton today has some 2,800 residents, the village population is only about 185, limited by lack of space for new homes.

Starting again at the north end of Afton, we see the first addition in the triangle of land between the fork of St. Croix Trail and Stagecoach Trail. This house was built by August Roodel in 1902 for his son Charles. Across from the Roodel place to the west on Stagecoach Trail, two more houses have sprung up. First north is the Arthur Clemens house, lived in also by his son Phil Clemens and family. Arthur Clemens was descended from Samuel Clemens from Hannibal, Missouri, a river town much like Afton.

Next to the Clemens house on the north is the Alfred "Bill" Swanlund house. Bill, the first mechanic in the Afton Garage, moved his house to this site from the south end of Afton following the great cloudburst of 1926.

Heading south on the west side of St. Croix Trail, beyond the former St. Paulus parsonage, we see the house built in 1902 and lived in by James and Sofia Nilsson Johnson for several years at the turn of the century. Johnson dug graves in Evergreen Cemetery on the hill. The Johnsons' daughter, Clara Johnson Clothier, also lived in this house, as did Myrta Morey Siebolds, mother-in-law of famed World War II correspondent Ernie Pyle.

At this point we discover, behind and west of the Johnson-Siebolds house, another new place. This house was built at the Spreeman Landing in the 1950s by new owner "Windmill Bill" Skluzacek and then moved here in the 1970s, far back from St. Croix Trail.

Back on St. Croix Trail, the many faceted former St. Croix Valley Academy was converted to a private residence by architect Robert Ackermann in 1965. Its three recently added decks soften the Spartan look of its tower.

Turning right onto Afton Boulevard, we see that the brown "Onion Pete" house has been remodeled but retains its essential 1880s appearance. The church parsonage next door, however, has been moved to 15945 St. Croix Trail. The old Afton Methodist Church itself housed a Washington County branch library in the 1980s; now painted a clean, bright blue, it is occupied as a studio and home by sculptor Arthur Norby and his wife.

Up on Pennington Avenue, our present tour reveals a street in great contrast to its rather undeveloped state in 1895. Now, along with a few remodeled older places, several new homes line the black-topped street and fill all the building sites.

The often-reworked old house on the west knoll now has brown shingles and is once again being remodeled. The pale green Rosenquist house, which we saw in 1895, is also extant. South of the Rosenquist house, the Afton Methodist Church built a new, split-level parsonage at 3296 Pennington in 1967. Today, it is occupied by St. Croix Valley United Methodist Church pastor, the Reverend John R. Darlington and his wife, Julie Andrews Darlington.

Just beyond the Methodist parsonage is the two-story Memorial Lutheran Church parsonage, built in 1963 under the pastorate of the Reverend Roger Mackey. The reason these two parsonages exist side-by-side goes back to 1855, when the men who platted Afton reserved property to be used for "school or church purposes." In 1980, however, the Lutherans sold their parsonage and it has since been owned by various individuals.

Next door, Harry "Beaver" Nordstrom built the little house to the south of the former Lutheran parsonage at 3322 Pennington in the early 1960s. Then, well west of the Nordstrom house, sidling up against the base of Mount Hope, a recent large A-frame home mirrors the morning sun from its great expanse of glass. At the corner where 34th Street intersects Pennington Avenue is a modern rambler constructed in 1957 by Earl and Lois Olmstead. A second story has recently expanded its size.

A short way west on 34th Street is the little house Harold "Jerry" and Hazel Briggs built after their marriage in 1933. It is being enlarged by its new owners. Just southeast and facing Pennington Avenue is the George Briggs, Sr. house, one of the very few Pennington places we noted on our 1895 tour. This old farmhouse has undergone many changes: Afton native Tom Johnson did the final, attractive modernization before selling it to its present owner. Next alongside the Briggs house is a 1960s split-level home, the last one south on Pennington's west side.

As our tour covers mainly the old village, we will skip Afton Coulee Ridge Road, developed originally by Schmitt Music president Robert A. Schmitt in the early 1970s and lying just outside the village's western boundary. Its six fine homes cling tenaciously to the hill south of the road to Mount Hope.

The southernmost house on the east side of Pennington is a one-story redwood rambler built in 1957 when there were only six other homes on that entire hill. From here back to the north end of Pennington, all of the seven homes on the east side may be called "new," constructed in the middle 1960s or later.

Down on Perrot Avenue, the Peter Paulson place and Swanson-Kallstrom house have been joined by the Paul Frederick house, now blue with white trim, which was moved to the corner of 32nd Street and Perrot some time after 1910, the year Frederick sold his store to Swan Pearson. Storekeeper Pearson lived in the next door parsonage, now "the little red house," formerly occupied by Rev. Simon Putnam.

Replacing the Frederick house near the corner of St. Croix Trail and Afton Blvd. for many years was a handsome two-story house erected in the 1920s by Albin Carlson who owned the Carlson Funeral Homes in St. Paul. Carlson sold the house to his brother-in-law Charlie Anderson who lived in it with his wife Hilma, whose sister was married to Carlson. One of the most attractive residences in Afton, it burned in June 1947, prompting citizens to organize the Afton Volunteer Fire Department, predecessor of the present Lower St. Croix Valley Fire Department. Long gone, too, is the Frederick-Pearson-Hayner store, razed about 1930.

Across 32nd Street, the 1857 Thomas-Johnson-Anderson house is now occupied by Mary Ann Scroggins, owner of the Afton Toy Shop. The blacksmith shop has departed long

AFTON'S OLDEST HOUSE WAS BUILT BY IRISH LUMBERMAN ANDREW MACKEY, WHO IN 1841 CLAIMED LAND IN WHAT IS NOW DOWNTOWN AFTON. IN 1855 HE SOLD HIS FARM TO THE FOUNDERS OF AFTON.

ago, but in 1960 Beryl Anderson Blomgren built behind the Thomas house on Perrot Avenue and nudging the westward bluff, a small, stylish duplex that is the only one in Afton.

The original Mackey house on St. Croix Trail with its white picket fence houses two businesses. Turning right on 33rd Street, we find a relatively recent place—the neat, white stucco house Clarence and Lorraine Lind built in 1949. Next to it is the Swan Hallberg house, which seems eternally waiting for rescue, its green roofing nearly gone.

Back on St. Croix Trail we see again the 1890 two-story Richert house, painted bright yellow with white trim. The lot next door where the Richert-Peterson-Pothen store stood is now part of the Squire House Gardens, which operates out of the former Squires residence on the next corner. The only vestige of the Richert store is an old ice shed about mid-block. Mildred Hipp enlarged the Squires house in the 1980s when she operated a gift and interior decorating business there and lived upstairs.

West of the Squires house, on 34th Street, the 1876 brick school has lost its bell tower as a private residence. Next door, at the base of the hill, is a small, neat colonial house built in the 1960s.

Afton Town Square has been upgraded for the 1990s with playground equipment, picnic tables, a basketball court, and a gazebo. An earlier pavilion, built by Nels Rosenquist for the American Legion about 1920, once dominated the park but collapsed under heavy snow a few years later.

South of Afton Town Square, the Getchell-Slater house, though altered, still resembles its original configuration. Gone for at least sixty years, however, is the store next door managed by Charles Getchell and George Slater, among others. The last proprietor of this business handling both groceries and hardware was Nels Lind. Part of the store's cement work is still visible where the building abutted the walkway.

At St. Croix Trail and 35th Street, the 1859 Joseph Dernley house has been well-preserved into the 1990s; painted tan with cream trim, it has a new enclosed porch.

Heading west on 35th Street, we find that wagon maker Andrew Sjoholm's house has burned and been replaced by a new one at 15882 35th Street. The John and Nellie Peterson house across the street has also been replaced by a brick rambler. The yellow Johnson-Spreeman house, however, still survives, situated well back from St. Croix Trail and under improvement by the present owners.

The Joseph Wolf Saloon, which stood east and north, close by the Johnson-Spreeman house, has now disappeared; moved to a new location, the old saloon now houses Lerk's Bar and Grill. Also gone is the Wolf Community Hall, sometimes called the Afton Auditorium Hall, built in 1906 on the north side of the creek and taken down in 1920. A tall hedge masks the site of this hall which once added richly to Afton's social life.

Crossing the bridge over the creek and turning west on 36th Street, we spot a white, barn-like building which was Emil Asp's blacksmith shop, established in 1910 and operating into the 1920s. Asp shod horses, sharpened plow shares, and made runners for sleighs. Farther west on the same street is a gray-blue, shingled house built in 1936. This marks the approximate site, we think, of the first school in Afton Village. Owner Rick Pung also holds title to the Asp blacksmith shop. Interestingly, a cement slab behind Pung's house hints an older structure likely existed there. The deed to this property, dating to 1851, carries the names of such early settlers as Andrew Mackey, Ralzamen Haskell, Hewit L. Thomas, Joseph Haskell, Charles Getchell, Nels Granberg, and Herbert Holberg.

The entry to Kel's Coulee—called Gummeson's Coulee a century ago—today reveals a large, two-story house built by Inter-State Lumber yard manager Elof Hallquist about 1910. Deep within the glen, the two nineteenth-century houses have been much lived in, remodeled, and enlarged. Behind and a bit west of the old Hallquist house at 3750 Pennington—on the lower level of that avenue—stands a modified A-frame home built in 1972 by Bruce and Julie Hallquist Peterson and now owned by Mike Rice and Dianne Hark.

Walking east out of the coulee, we find on our right the Thorvald Holberg place unchanged on the outside but renovated inside. Next to the Holberg residence is a house that Richard Johnson, an enthusiastic Boy Scoutmaster, moved from Pennington to this 36th Street location. On Pennington, it had been occupied a few years by the Peter Fredericksons who were related to the Rosenquists. This neat, gray house is now home to Johnson's son Kevin Johnson and his family. Next door to the Johnsons is another relatively new rambler.

At the corner of St. Croix Trail and 36th Street, the 1882 Milbert Clymer house has been added onto over the years. Also remaining on St. Croix Trail and 37th Street, painted white with smart, black trim, is the 1857 home of shingle-maker Asa Tracy. West of it on 37th Street we find two recent houses snuggled into the valley of heavy woods at the base of the hill, one on the north side, the other on the south.

On St. Croix Trail again, we see the beautiful "Spruce Hill" home, now painted yellow, still presiding over the southern end of the village from its vantage point among the pines.

A bit south of 37th Street, there was once a public water trough that supplied artesian water from springs in the hills. Horses drank from the trough while citizens cupped their hands where the water was conveyed through a pipe. Afton resident Phyllis Rosenquist Fredrickson wrote that "This water was the sweetest water this side of heaven." In 1926 a cloudburst brought down soil from the hilltops and buried the trough in silt and mud. Its usefulness had peaked during the era when Afton relied on horses for transportation.

At the southern limits of the village, the Charles V. Johnson house stands behind a trim fence at the foot of the hill. As solid as ever, it is occupied by Kenneth Johnson, one of C.V.'s grandsons, and his family. Charlie's daughter, Bernadine "Sis" Holberg, said that her father once sold farm implements and machinery from the Afton Garage when he lived in this house.

Turning around and heading north again, we find that the first house on the east is a relatively new one. But the little Nord-Swanson house next door to the north has been occupied continuously since 1880. The 1859 Jenny Peters-Magnus Hedstrom house, blue with cream trim, is another survivor. North of the creek, Ole Thueson's little house has outlived its questionable past.

The next place north turns out to be the old Methodist Church parsonage, formerly located on Afton Boulevard, which was moved here to 15945 So. St. Croix Trail in the 1980s, replacing the Sill-Greer house.

Turning east and crossing the old railroad bed—the rails were removed soon after the train's last run in 1978—we see the little Otto Parson house by the river, somewhat the worse for wear because of its many renters, but now being restored. Opposite it, replacing Fred Korth's house, is the two-story house built by Afton native Leonard Nordstrom.

Back on St. Croix Trail, we have learned the next house was a second one constructed by wagon maker Andrew Sjoholm. His granddaughter, Dorothy Hayner Riedell, told us Sjoholm constructed this two-story house that her family, the Joe Hayners, lived in. This blue house has been home to the Kerschbaum family for many years.

GEORGE AND MINNIE STONE SLATER AT HOME ON WASHINGTON STREET (NOW ST. CROIX TRAIL). GEORGE WAS STOREKEEPER-POSTMASTER AT THE GETCHELL-BUILT STORE SOUTH OF THE PARK. HE RENTED MY PARENTS THEIR HONEYMOON COTTAGE AT ST. MARY'S POINT.

The next stop north is a small clearing with a sign reading "Steamboat Park;" unfortunately, no shoreline restoration of the old landing has taken place.

Back on the main street, the 1880s structure known as Selma's is still full of life, having done duty as an ice cream parlor, beer and sandwich tavern, bait shop, and post office. Next to Selma's, the George Benson place appears timeless, but Chris Christensen's blacksmith shop, which had appeared shaky for many years, was finally razed in March 1996.

The little blue bungalow with attached breezeway at 3395 So. St. Croix Trail was built by Dana Judson and Rachel Squires Peabody; Rachel was the daughter of Frank and Emma Rosenquist Squires who lived across the street for many years. East of the Peabody house remain Afton's two Indian mounds. But where the Picullel house formerly stood crowding the Peabody house is now a small, open greensward.

THE MARTIN LIND
FAMILY. BACK ROW,
LEFT TO RIGHT: GENE,
CASPER, BENNIE,
CLIFFORD. FRONT ROW:
MARTIN (FATHER), RUSS
HAROLD (LERK),
CLARENCE, EMMA
(MOTHER), MERLE.

In the middle 1980s the Afton Historical Society with laudable ambition planned to move the Picullel place to the park in Afton. Unfortunately, its old-fashioned construction made the plan unworkable, and it finally had to be razed.

Next to where the Picullel house stood, the green concrete block building built in 1917 as a commercial garage and Ford dealership today shelters the Afton Post Office. The two gas pumps which stood along the street were removed in the 1950s. Across the alleyway is the tiny structure barber Herbert Sill moved from behind the Getchell-Slater house for his barber shop, also in 1917. The building was wrestled onto skids and dragged there by horses.

Next door stands the old Wolf Saloon, now Lerk's Bar, which Bert Johnson and Ervin Peterson moved here from the south end of the village in 1920 for a confectionery store during Prohibition. Harold "Lerk" Lind established his hamburger and tavern business here by the early 1940s. Harold was called Lerk, which means onion in Swedish, because he had picked so many onions as a boy; his famous hamburgers with onions became known as "Lerkburgers."

The brick bank building on the corner was built in 1913 and now houses various businesses. Behind the bank, the Afton Berry Shed flourished from 1914 to 1935, but was not demolished until after the 1965 flood. Across 33rd Street, Gordie and Kathy Jarvis's Afton House Inn has evolved from the 1867 Cushing Hotel. Somewhere deep within the structure is an even older building—the little house Miner Thomas built in 1859. On the next corner, at 32nd Street, the diminutive 1855 shelter Meredith Thomas turned into a store has also disappeared and become part of a new, large house that contains a gift and interior decorating business.

Strolling east on 32nd Street, we find a low, one-story gray house built by Bert Spreeman in 1941. To keep a twenty-four-hour watch on his fishing boat business, he had placed the house near the shore, but high water and ice after a few seasons forced him to move it west over the railroad tracks to its present site.

Continuing down 32nd Street, we find at the former Spreeman Landing a veritable city of docks and canopied slips sheltering luxury craft, row after row along the waterfront. This is the Windmill Marina, named by marina owner Bill Skluzacek for the windmill Bert Spreeman had erected to pump cold river water into his minnow tank.

On the north side of 32nd Street, as we head back toward St. Croix Trail, a driveway leads to Jerry Schottmuller's new rambler at the edge of the old pasture. Schottmuller makes his living in a woodshop on the site where he repairs furniture and makes cabinets.

Crossing the 1971 dike east of the old railroad bed, we see once more the 1859 house built by Charles Getchell, changed very little over the years. Willie Johnson lived here many years.

FRANK SPREEMAN'S FISH SHOP ON WASHINGTON STREET, JUST SOUTH OF THE FORMER CONGREGATIONAL CHURCH.

Up on the corner of St. Croix Trail and 32nd Street, the Spreeman octagon house is no more! Spreading out behind the well-trimmed hedge is a spacious yard belonging to the little bungalow Emil "Spike" Spreeman built after dismantling his parents' historic house in 1944. The Spreeman fish market, which lay a few steps north of the house, came down at the same time.

Next door to the fish market site stands the little city garage. Built in 1948 as a fire barn by Afton's Volunteer Fire Department, it now stores a lawn mower, snow-blower, and other maintenance equipment. Alongside the garage the 1868 Congregational church building is now the Afton Historical Museum, renovated for that function in 1987. Its front entry has been re-designed; its new orange-yellow color harmonizes happily with its New England ancestry.

Around the corner, pressed close to the museum at 15909 Afton Blvd., is the former Clifford and Eunice Anderson cottage, moved here in 1944 from its original location south of the Spreeman Landing.

Across Afton Blvd. on St. Croix Trail, the house occupied by Rev. W. D. Ahl of the Lutheran Seminary has new siding and an enclosed porch. Afton Methodist Church pillars Lawrence "Shorty" Johnson and his wife Linda Hallquist Johnson were longtime residents, and the house now shelters the Johnsons' granddaughter and her family. East of this house on Afton Blvd. remains the 1882 Swenson-Spreeman-Kane house, in which Henry and Marion Mullen Kane lived for many recent years. Today it is home to a young family typical of so many others adopting Afton in their quest for quietude.

Turning north on Pike Avenue, we come to a 1970s rambler built by Ella Spreeman Johnson behind the site of the old lumber yard. The lumber yard property itself, fronting St. Croix Trail at 31st Street, is now occupied by Afton Market Square, humming with a variety of new business ventures within an attractive little mall.

Actually, Afton has had three lumber yards on this same property. The first one burned prior to 1900, and another was built to replace it. This second yard was owned by Inter-State Lumber Company and managed by Paul Bahneman and then Elof Hallquist. Notable because Andersen Corporation pioneer Fred Andersen learned his earliest lessons about wood here, this yard also burned, about 1944.

The third lumber yard, another Inter-State business, was under the management of that unflappable old German, Henry Sommer, who also served a stint as mayor of the village. Inter-State finally fell to competition from other yards in 1988, and its deteriorating building was remodeled several years later as the present Afton Market Square.

Turning around at the corner of 31st Street, we head east to the edge of the old pasture where Afton's train, fondly dubbed the "Peanut," ran for ninety-six years. Now, the freight trains and passenger trains, the depot, coal sheds, windmill-water tank, and grain elevator have all given way to a second Afton marina—the Afton Marina and Yacht Club, a cooperative association of boat owners.

Walking back west on 31st Street to Pike Avenue, we find a handsome, two-story log house erected in the late 1980s. West of it on St. Croix Trail is the old Martin Lind house, which has seen better times. North of the Lind house on St. Croix Trail is a colonial-style house built in 1946 by returning World War II veteran and Afton native George "Judd" Eastwood, who in the 1950s became Afton's mayor. Judd's grandparents, the Thomas Eastwoods, as well as his wife Catherine's grandparents, the Ferdinand Richerts, figured prominently in Afton's early history. Our last stop on this tour is the 1982 Afton City Hall. The nerve center of the city, it is across the street from the St. Paulus German Lutheran parsonage—about where we started our two tours. These two sites, nearly ninety years apart in their beginnings, one sacred and the other secular, neatly frame much of Afton's past.

AFTON'S SECOND RAILROAD DEPOT, BUILT IN THE EARLY 1940S. PICTURED ARE AGENT TED LARSON AND HIS NEPHEW KENNETH OPSAHL.

AMONG HER AMENITIES

Afton perhaps never lived up to the expectations of its founders; it never became a commercial crossroads of any importance. But perhaps it has become something better as Aftonites, past and present, have preserved the rural character of this idyllic hamlet.

For preservation on a grand scale, we need look no farther than the Valley Creek area of Afton. There one of education's premier achievements, the Belwin Outdoor Education Laboratory, was created by the large vision and generosity of retired General Mills chairman Charles H. Bell.

It all began simply enough. In the winter of 1970 Bell bought sixty-seven acres of Valley Creek property for a retreat and built a small cabin. Realizing the need for a buffer zone around this property, he and his wife Lucy and their daughter Lucy Hartwell began adding to the original purchase. The Belwin property today totals more than one thousand acres.

Charlie Bell had nothing more on his mind at first than protecting this pristine land so near the Twin Cities from development. But with the acreage accumulating, his wife and daughter began asking him what he intended to do with all of it. One option was to keep this place of solace and beauty for his family, of course. Then again, he discussed offering it to the University of Minnesota as a long-range environmental research outpost, and even investigated its possible use by the Hennepin County Park Reserve District.

While exploring various alternatives, Bell was introduced to Rod Frye, a former Glacier National Park ranger and St. Paul public school teacher. It was a fortuitous meeting. Frye had been given the job of locating a property where St. Paul public school teachers could teach a variety of disciplines in an "outdoor environmental laboratory." Bell sensed at once the excitement of the concept. "This was one of those serendipitous meetings in life when you say immediately, 'You're right,'" he remembered.

THE SNUG RETREAT CHARLES BELL BUILT FOR HIS FAMILY AT VALLEY CREEK IS NOW SURROUNDED BY THE OUTDOOR ENVIRONMENTAL LABORATORY HE DEVELOPED FOR SCHOOL CHILDREN.

111

Belwin's cooperative arrangement with the St. Paul public schools is unique. The property is owned and maintained by the Belwin Foundation, while the school system provides the educational programs and staff. Some employees are Belwin staff members while others work for the St. Paul public school system. The handsome Belwin Center building was constructed under Charlie Bell's direction by Afton resident Elton "Blackie" Hancock.

Belwin (the name combines Bell with Winton, Lucy Bell's maiden name) welcomed its first students in November 1971. Rod Frye became Belwin's first educational director, and Dr. Benny "Doc" Kettelkamp, another veteran Glacier Park ranger and retired University of Wisconsin professor of biology, served as environmental director for thirteen years. They made an ideal team in teaching respect for the land. "They sang off the same song sheet," commented current environmental coordinator Janice Odegaard.

For the past twenty-five years, 10,000 to 12,000 children have visited Belwin annually. Typically, large classes are divided into small groups of students who are accompanied by their teacher and a Belwin volunteer on the outdoor trails. This is where much valuable instruction takes place. "If the teacher is creative enough, he or she can use nature to teach almost anything," said Kettlekamp.

Belwin's impact upon children, especially those from urban St. Paul, is often surprising and touching. Some youngsters who have never entered woods are fearful of encountering bears. Others, seeing so much sky at once, are full of wonder. A few to whom silence is almost unknown burst into tears when they first experience it. "One little lamb," remarked Odegaard, "asked the educational director, 'Are you Mother Nature?'"

Walking through the snow and feeling it drift softly through the pines can be another unfamiliar experience. In the city, snow is an inconvenience—something to be shoveled away. At Belwin, Robert Frost's poem "Stopping by Woods on a Snowy Evening" comes alive as nowhere else. Similarly, the birds, butterflies, and prairie grasses provide powerful empathy with the early settlers of the St. Croix Valley. In Belwin's "Enchanted Forest," children sit on log benches and write poetry or watch a play performed by their peers in an outdoor amphitheater amidst this profusion of nature.

Maintaining the natural habitat and preserving eleven at-risk ecosystems within the Belwin property (a native prairie area, a beaver work area, a geological drift area, and a woodland pothole, to name a few) is an on-going and immense challenge. "With a big tract like this, you can't just freeze the land in time," explained Odegaard. "You must do something with it, or it will change of its own accord and often in ways you don't want."

Diseased trees are removed, for instance, and each spring managed burns restore and maintain the prairie areas. Without the burns, plant diversity would be lost to invading woody plants. With this invasion would come a loss of animal species which now include deer, foxes, beavers, badgers, otters, wild turkeys, ducks, geese, herons, and bald eagles. Belwin also works to improve conditions for threatened and endangered species including the Blandings Turtle.

From the start, Charles Bell knew that Belwin would benefit from broadly based support. He was no longer young and wanted the project to be his legacy. He therefore enlisted the help of acquaintances, friends, and foundations who shared his environmental views and were willing to back them financially. At the entry to the Belwin lodge stands a large, gray rock with a bronze plaque listing the names of the original donors. Above the names, Bell wrote, "These people cared enough about students to make the dream of Belwin a reality."

CHARLES H. AND LUCY WINTON BELL.

In 1973 "Friends of Belwin" was organized to expand the number of supporters to include St. Croix Valley residents who also saw the value in this unique educational venture and appreciated its location in the Afton area.

Belwin staff members with the longest terms of service include custodian Larry Cline, property manager John Palmen, and naturalist Bruce Albrecht. Two other local veterans, now retired, were the late Joyce Sommerdorf, property manager, and secretary Carol Milano. The present education director is Karen Casper.

Charlie Bell takes a great deal of satisfaction from watching school children interacting with nature. From them, he speculates, may emerge some who will join his crusade to protect the land against exploitation. The mission of Charles Bell and his family through this priceless project has been no less than to foster within people, young and old alike, a lifelong stewardship of our threatened world.

AFTON'S FOURTH OF JULY PARADE GOING BOTH WAYS: ON THE LEFT, HEADING SOUTH ON ST. CROIX TRAIL, DON GROTH IS DRIVING HIS 1921 MODEL T FORD TOURING CAR. RETURNING NORTH ALONG THE SAME ROUTE IS LUCY McALLISTER'S AFTON SCHOONER BAND.

Come the Fourth of July each year, Afton residents celebrate their pride of place with one of the most unusual parades anywhere. Because Afton's main street is only a few blocks long, the parade lines up at the Afton Market Square building at the north end of town, marches the half mile or so to the south end of town, then turns around and returns along the same route to where it started. Towards the end of the parade, you can watch it going and coming at the same time.

Afton's earliest Fourth of July celebration dates back to the late 1800s, but for many years the parade was discontinued. It was happily resurrected in 1975 as a much-needed rehearsal for the next year's Bicentennial event. Vice-presidential candidate Walter Mondale was the grand marshal in 1976, accompanied by Lucy McAllister and her Afton Schooner Band. Residents had so much fun that they have continued the

114

parade every year since. Long-time resident Don Groth drives the grand marshal in one or another of his restored cars, parade chairman Richard Eisinger, dressed as Paul Revere, rides one of his trusty steeds, and citizens of all ages and even their pets join in, some riding on homemade floats, others walking or riding bicycles or driving all manner of motorized vehicles.

Following the parade, spectators swarm into Afton Town Square for a long afternoon of loud music, children's games, talent contests, pop, beer, and brats. Scarcely anyone in Afton escapes contributing to the day's noisy success. Overflowing with small town warmth and neighborliness, Afton's Fourth of July celebrations need only Norman Rockwell to capture their exuberance.

Other annual events include the Afton Village Fair each May, when main street merchants welcome spring with entertainment and sidewalk sales; Selma's 10-K Run in September; and Art in the Park in October. Begun in 1978 by a group of women led by librarian and weaver Lois Arnold, Art in the Park is a juried show and sale in Afton Town Square.

Tourists are always entranced by the variety of small, neat shops within the former Afton Village, some of them snugged into historic structures, lending them a crowded but appealing antiquity. There's "the little red house," for example, in Rev. Simon Putnam's parsonage; Squire House Gardens in the former Squires residence; and several small businesses including an inviting coffee shop in the former bank building.

In recent years Afton was without a grocery store until several dozen younger citizens banded together to effect a solution to this sorry situation. The happy result of their efforts is the Afton Village Co-op, which opened in 1994 in the refurbished Afton Market Square Building. Attorney Jim Gasperini was the mastermind behind converting the old Inter-State Lumber Company building into this attractive mini-mall.

In addition to a spurt of new businesses, Afton is now served by two publications. *The Afton Citizens' Forum Bulletin*, begun in 1968 with the encouragement and financial aid of John and Grace Stoltze, keeps citizens informed about city council and planning commission meetings as well as other city business. Then in 1991 Peggy Gunderson launched *The Afton Paper* to cover not only local government but more general and folksy news as well. An earlier Afton paper, the *Afton Courier* published by B.F. Stanley, did not survive beyond its first issue in June, 1880; largely a flowery paean to Afton's natural beauty, this first newspaper can be seen at the Afton Historical Museum.

Especially proud is Afton of its active historical society and handsome museum exhibiting a remarkable variety of farm tools, artifacts, and photographs. Capturing nineteenth-century life in this early river town, museum displays detail an existence

largely forgotten. The dream of two former Twin Citians, David and Gloria Haslund, the Afton Historical Museum celebrated its grand opening in the old city hall with appropriate ceremonies in June 1988. Gloria is president of the Afton Historical Society. The museum is capably managed by curator Sandy Berglund and her assistant Judy Osborn.

Summing up any city is like trying to hold running water in one's hands. Just when we think we understand a bit about it, another change occurs, a new facet of character is revealed. But since Afton to date has had no written history, it seemed to me a challenge worth meeting. Afton, after all, is in my blood.

After having been a "summer person" from the age of four, I finally achieved my longtime dream of becoming a full-timer following World War II in 1947. Joining in the mink ranching business with my brother Dave Robb and his brother-in-law Bruce Johnson, an Afton native, I gradually grew closer to the town and its residents. Membership in the little Afton Methodist Church brought more of the same.

Today from the windows of my home on Afton's western bluff below the higher Mount Hope, I can look across the river to Rattlesnake Hill or "the sleeping elephant," as we children called it, with its trunk forming Catfish Bar's long slender strand. It was there that I spent long, sunny days with my young friends of summer—always beside, on, or in the clear, tannish water.

Now, too, with the rooftops of old Afton Village partially visible through the forest net below my house, I can see the town laid out in front of me. I can see, too, in imagination many of those long-gone folks, kindly and gentle, many of them poor, who people Afton's history. Often from other lands, they gave Afton some of her sweetness. And loved her as deeply as I always will.

BIBLIOGRAPHY

Baumgart, Reuben, "First Swede Lived in Valley Creek," in *Memorial Lutheran Church Footprints*, Afton, Minnesota. Vol. 3, No.1, March 1985.

Blegen, Theodore C., *Minnesota Farmers' Diaries, William R. Brown, 1845-46, Mitchell Y. Jackson, 1852-63*. The Minnesota Historical Society, St. Paul, Minnesota, 1939.

Comfort, Mildred Houghton, *Meet Tom Cooney*. The Lund Press, Minneapolis, Minnesota, 1945.

Dunn, James Taylor, *The St. Croix River: Midwest Border River*. Holt, Rinehard, Winston, New York, N.Y., 1965.

Dieter, Richard, "This Afton," in *The Afton Citizens' Forum Bulletin*. Afton, Minnesota. Bulletins 82, 91, 92, 95, 137, March 1976–September 1981.

Easton, Augustus B., *History of the Saint Croix Valley*. H.C. Cooper, Jr. and Company, Chicago, Illinois, 1909.

Folsom, W.H.C., *Fifty Years in the Northwest*. Pioneer Press Company, St. Paul, Minnesota, 1888.

Francis, Dola; Robb, Babette; Haslund, Gloria; Torgerson, Wynona P.; Sybrant, Marylyn, *A St. Croix Valley Story*. The Croixside Press, Stillwater, Minnesota, 1972.

Grant, Evelyn Bolles, *History of Valley Creek and Surrounding Afton Township*, Afton, Minnesota, January 1963.

Gunning, Lu and Bev Wychor, St. Peter Lutheran Committee, *St. Peter Lutheran Church of Afton, 1863-1988: 125 Years of God's Blessing—Our Heritage for Tomorrow*, 1988.

Haskell, Hiram A., *Joseph Haskell of Afton*, Limited Edition by Hiram A. Haskell, M.D., Windsor, California, May 1941.

Neill, Edward D., *History of Washington County and the St. Croix River Valley*. North Star Publishing, Minneapolis, Minnesota, 1881.

Palm, Harry W., *Lumberjack Days*. Bayport Printing House, Inc., Bayport, Minnesota, 1969.

Robb, Esther Chapman, *History of the Afton Methodist Church, 1854-1954*. Star-Observer Publishing Company, Hudson, Wisconsin, 1954.

_____, "The Swede-Indian," in *The American Swedish Historical Foundation Yearbook* for 1960. Philadelphia, Pennsylvania.

Roen, Christine, *Goodly Heritage: The Story of Memorial Lutheran Church*. North Central Publishing Company, St. Paul, Minnesota, 1982.

Rosenfelt, Willard, editor. *Washington: A History of the County*. Croixside Press, Stillwater, Minnesota, 1977.

In addition, we are indebted to the following newspaper columnists: Alvin Hedstrom in the *Stillwater Gazette*, and Gareth Hiebert, Ben Kern, and Mary Perkins in the *St. Paul Pioneer Press*.

INDEX

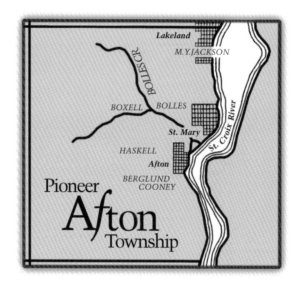

Lakeland
M.Y.JACKSON

BOLLES CR.

BOXELL   BOLLES

St. Mary

St. Croix River

HASKELL
Afton
BERGLUND
COONEY

Pioneer
Afton
Township

Designed by
Barbara J. Arney

Typeface is
Trump Medieval

Archival photos restored by designer
using electronic imaging